Hollywoo[d]

Everything You Need to Know Before Moving to Los Angeles

Andy Wasif

ISBN: 151226850X
ISBN-13: 978-1512268508

Cover photo by Mikul Robins www.mikulphotography.net
Cover design by Bogdan Matei www.elance.com/s/edit/cascadorys

For more of Andy Wasif's work, visit www.wasifsworld.com.

TABLE OF CONTENTS

INTRODUCTION

Congratulations! You have made a momentous decision to follow your dream and move to Los Angeles. (And the secondary decision to purchase this book which, let's be frank, will be far more integral to your growth as a human being.) There's plenty of room here for you. (There really isn't, but since this conversation should've been had in the late 80s, it's too late to do anything about it now. One more person isn't going to make a difference.) So . . . welcome!

From wherever you are moving, you will find that Los Angeles is a city like no other. Much of that is because Hollywood is an industry like no other. The two are interconnected, and you will find it all totally disconcerting.

When you first move to LA, expect to feel uncomfortable with its cultural idiosyncrasies. Then, after a few years, you'll get used to it. In fact, it might seem even more disconcerting when you begin to dismiss all these quirks as normal. It's only when you visit other cities that you'll remember how messed up LA is. Not to say this is bad, but it's an acquired taste, like chopped liver. (On a side note, I still refuse to eat chopped liver.)

The purpose of this book is to go beyond every one of the questions you have before you move to Los Angeles. Perhaps you've had the basics answered in a film class, from a friend who has lived here for a few years, or from watching all eight seasons of Entourage. These questions may include: How do I break into the business? How are the waves along the Malibu shorelines? What kind of job can I get while still pursuing auditions? Are there any places I can get a good pizza pie? What are the best places to network or be seen?

This book tells you how to LIVE in Los Angeles, how to NAVIGATE the industry, and how to THRIVE in your profession. It answers the questions you don't ask because you wouldn't think these questions needed to be asked.

LA is a unique place and this transcends its geographic coordinates, referring also to the manner in which people interact and the vibe as a whole. The industry itself is all a game and, in order to beat the game, you have to know the game.

If you're still on the fence about moving, there is a school of thought that says you can make it in Hollywood regardless of where in the world you live. I, however, subscribe to the theory that if you want to get sick, hang around sick people. (And really, is there anyone sicker than Hollywood types? I kid, I kid.)

Would you go to Memphis, Tennessee to make it in politics? Or Washington, DC to record your breakthrough album? Yes, it's true, you can be creative from anywhere, especially with the Interweb. Even a Tibetan monk who has taken a vow of silence can sell a sitcom based on his hilarious tweets on the wackiness down at the monastery. Nevertheless, your odds of success in the business are better when you live here.

Throughout this book, I'm going to speak in generalities as much as possible. Take everything I say with a grain of salt. These examples come from either my individual experiences or from recurring conversations I've had with friends who have spent ample time in Hollywood, enough to endorse and verify these statements. (And by "friends", I mean people who I truly know very little about other than how we met, what vocation they're trying to succeed in, and, from time to time, a personal fact such as a spouse's name or where they grew up.)

That said, this book may be full of crap when you weigh it against all the other things you've heard, but all I can do is speak for what seems to be the consensus. Your ultimate experience may be nothing like this, in which case, you can write your own book someday.

So now, without any further ado, here is your initiation into the culture that is Hollywood. May all your dreams come true! Insert chapter one text here.

CHAPTER 1 - THE BASICS

INTRO
Since you'll be calling Los Angeles home for a while, you should probably know the specs on your house to give you an idea of what you'll be dealing with and not seem like such a rube.

FACTS
Actually, this may teach you more about the city than most of the residents know. Don't worry if you forget these little nuggets; there will not be a test.

Population
The city itself *only* houses close to 3.9 million people. (Did writing "only" make you think it was a small city?) This does not include the whole region. The county of Los Angeles contains 10.02 million people according to the 2013 census. It's a safe bet that this is more than the county from where you are coming.

Nickname
They call Greater Los Angeles "the Southland", even though San Diego is farther *south* of it. Who knows what they call San Diego? Truth is, no one here cares.

Counties
Los Angeles is in Los Angeles County (Duh!). "The Southland" includes five counties: Los Angeles, Riverside, San Bernadino, San Gabriel, and Orange County. South of that is San Diego County.

Airports

The airports to which you will become most familiar are Los Angeles International Airport and Burbank Airport. There are a couple outside the city such as John Wayne Airport and LA/Ontario Airport but, chances are, you won't be flying into or out of those. (Do you get the feeling if you're a big enough star someday, they'll just name an airport after you?)

Los Angeles International Airport (LAX)

LAX is the major international airport in town. Much of the time, it's seven terminals of pure chaos. Leave yourself time because you never know how long the line getting through security is going to take. I've made it from my bedroom to the gate in a record 25 minutes, but I've also been stuck in the ticketing line for an hour and missed my flight. You'll have to get a sense of peak and off-peak times.

Security is tight, so when you drop someone off, pull over, pop the trunk, dump their luggage out, and get out of there. Let's go, people! MOVE IT!!!

Burbank Bob Hope Airport (BUR)

Burbank equals fewer flight options compared to the airport of any major city, but it is such a cakewalk. You'll enter the one-level facility, go through security and make the short walk to your gate in no time. You almost want to just hang out there for a day as it's so calm and relaxed.

John Wayne Airport (SNA)

This is also an international airport, but it is in Orange County. If you happen to live south of LAX, this presents a good alternative down in the town of Santa Ana.

LA/Ontario Airport (ONT)

Not to be left out of the whole international airport racket, San Bernadino has its own, just outside the town of Ontario along the 10 freeway. It's still also commonly known as Ontario International

Airport and if you live along the eastern border of Los Angeles, (Pasadena, perhaps?), maybe this is the airport for you.

Long Beach Airport (LGB)
Finally, nestled among the 405, the 710, and the 605, the LBC has an airport with an old school feel to it. You walk along the tarmac and up the stairs where Pan Am stewardesses kiss you on the cheek as you board. (I'm not sure this actually happens as I've never been to this airport.) It's also the West Coast hub for JetBlue Airways.

Time Zone
Los Angeles is in the Pacific Time Zone, three hours behind the Eastern Time Zone. It is also three hours ahead of Hawaii. Sometimes it's an hour behind Arizona, sometimes it's not. This is just how Arizona screws with us.

City Hall
The mayor of Los Angeles is Eric Garcetti.

City Anthem
Yes, LA has an anthem. It's *I Love LA* by Randy Newman and is played at Dodgers Stadium after a Dodgers win. You will hear the song quite often on the radio too. It's a tongue-in-cheek look at the car-cruising, sun-worshipping, oblivious culture that is LA. It's not meant to be an insult, as Newman himself has said, "There's some kind of ignorance LA has that I'm proud of . . ." but it doesn't matter because most people don't pay attention to any of the words outside of when to yell out "*We love it!*"

GEOGRAPHY
Reno is actually *west* of Los Angeles, longitudinally-speaking. LA County juts out toward Japan before heading north to San Francisco or south to San Diego, making it more of an east-west coastline.

The Landscape

You are in the mountains. Many people do not realize that Los Angeles is the most mountainous city in California. (Suck on that, San Francisco!)

Therefore, hiking trails abound! Hiking may be the number one hobby of Los Angelenos. That's what the mountains are there for. Well, that and providing an impediment to traffic flow.

Palm Trees

Most of you will find an abundance of something you are not used to seeing on a daily basis and that is . . . palm trees. They are synonymous with Southern California, yet most of them are not indigenous to the region. Only one type of palm tree is native to California and that is the California fan palm. As this is not a book about palm trees, I will let you do your own research about the subject if you have nothing better to do with your time.

The Ocean

Los Angeles County lies against a coastline and, for this reason, one might imagine that Los Angeles is at sea level. In fact, most of it is *above* sea level but the famous Pacific Ocean draws a lot of notice, mainly because it is the largest ocean in the world. At the very least, it's in the top three. (No one can be sure because they keep losing measuring sticks when they try to check its size.) It gets pretty deep too, just not right at the shore.

There are many nice beaches up and down the coast, from Redondo Beach to Malibu, with lots of spots in between. The water is swimmable and surfable. Yes, there are some places where it's probably best not to let the water touch your skin, and you should never *ingest* the ocean, but overall, you'll enjoy your time there. You may even see some dolphins frolicking.

And the beaches are walkable. There is lots of sand, much of which is littered with debris requiring local organizations and high school students to organize beach clean ups constantly but, overall, you'll feel like a regular cast member of *Baywatch* in no time.

The Hill

When people talk about "the hill", they are talking about the large land mass separating Los Angeles from "the valley". This is an area of contention; many people will not venture "over the hill", while many people love it there. There is no right answer . . . except the first one. That's the right answer.

"Over the hill" represents a more suburban, laid back way to live. And it's hot. Soooooooo much hotter.

Downtown LA

Downtown LA, or "DTLA" as it is often called, is located in the Eastern hemisphere of anywhere you'll most likely need to be. However, it's becoming more like a real city every day with events and destinations and the increasing reach of METRO's light rail system.

It's convenient for those who work downtown, however you'll find very few Hollywood creative types (besides artists) here. Chances are good that your first visit here will be when you have jury duty.

The LA River

Haha. Wait till you see this! (The joke is it's not so much a river as it is a cement aqueduct. But there's talk of a revitalization!)

CLIMATE

So why is LA the place to be in terms of climate? Essentially, you are in the desert. It rains very little and doesn't get too cold. Depending on how close you are to the ocean, it doesn't get too hot either. (The further inland you go, the hotter it gets. We're talking 120 degrees or so, but that's around Palm Springs or Death Valley. In the San Fernando Valley, you only have to worry about the low hundreds.)

When it gets hot, it can get very hot, very fast, but the good news is the humidity is typically low which means it's automatically ten degrees cooler in the shade. Just find the nearest tree and let the palm fronds give you a respite from the oppressive temps.

The days start cool and end cool with noticeable jumps and drops in the temps as you drive around town (with the "hill" providing a demarcation point between *It's hot!* and *Kill me now, it's hot!* Because of this, dressing in layers is your best bet. Flip flops are the footwear of choice because socks and shoes do not allow your feet to breathe.

As you may have heard, the climate is changing. It's raining less and less and getting drier and drier. There's no telling how much drier it will become. (Bring your own water when you get here. I would say enough for 5-6 years, just to be safe.) Summer usually takes place in the late summer through the fall, and then with select days here and there throughout the holiday season. (There will be three days in the middle of November when the temps spike to 90 after a run of days in the 60s.)

Don't worry about Grandma's knitted Thanksgiving and Christmas sweaters, either. You probably won't need to wear them as it's going to be warm enough for merely a thin pullover most of the time while still rocking your flip flops. (Winter coats? Only if you'll be hitting the slopes.)

Seasons

Perhaps you've caught word of the infamous seasonal variations here in Los Angeles. There is summer, then there is *notsomuch summer*. Maybe more like a *slightly less than spring*. In other words, there is one season.

I always feel this is one reason why you look back after living here for several years and can't believe how much time has passed. It's because you have no benchmarks like one snowfall after another. It all just blends together.

People will remark how "cold" it is outside when the temperatures plummet into the 60s. You'll scoff at them, at first. If you are from a cold-weather area and were used to running around outside in subzero temperatures wearing nothing but shorts and a tank top, there will come a time when your body acclimatizes. That means you'll start wearing a heavy sweater when it's 60 degrees and will get laughed at by your friends back home. It may not be today, it may not be tomorrow, but it'll happen. I'm from Canada and you should see my ensemble when it gets into the 60s.

You can expect unseasonably warm temps at times throughout the spring, as well.

Sunshine

If you want an easy job in Los Angeles without much variation, apply to be a meteorologist. (The only issue you'll have is what wacky name to take as all the popular ones in Los Angeles such as Dallas Raines or the retired Johnny Mountain are already in use.) For a good idea of just how consistently sunny Los Angeles is, watch *LA Story* as Steve Martin's weatherman just throws magnetic suns at the weather map.

Many people buy a screen they can leave on their windshield when they park to keep the inside of their car from becoming a convection oven. The sun is ruthless – and this is why parking spaces under the shade are the first to be taken.

Be careful not to leave anything important inside your car for too long as it'll soon become faded. The same goes for your left arm. (Yes, that's correct. Your *left* arm!) If you spend a lot of time in your car with your window open and your left arm resting on it, you will find it will become more tanned (burned?) than your right arm.

You'll never notice the sun more than when you are driving west during that afternoon commute. You're trying to negotiate the gridlocked traffic and horrific drivers *with* your sunglasses on while adjusting your visor, and you're *still* squinting. Since much of the city is laid out in a grid pattern and lined with reflective buildings, most of the major thoroughfares aimed directly at the sun have been reclassified as "death roads".

Smog

LA is typically No. 1 when it comes to the worst smog and ozone pollution in the country. For the longest time, I never bothered to look up where the term "smog" came from, but instead always assumed it just meant "smutty fog" because it's dirty and it's foggy. (It's actually a combo of "smoke" and "fog".)

It's also in the top five for producing pollutants. Expect high levels of particulate matter such as dust and soot (this does not include the bullshit that agents spew) at all times so, if you have allergies, chances are, they will be exacerbated. And if you wear contact lenses, they will give you more trouble. Sneezing will increase. Your sinuses will hate you. (Just keep telling them they won't have to shovel snow anymore.)

The liberal in me says that if you can get everyone to buy an electric car, we would not have that smog problem. But people need their status symbols like SUVs, gas guzzlers, etc. They feel they've done their part when they drive a hybrid SUV that now gets nine miles to the gallon instead of two.

All that being said, LA's smog levels *are* on the decline. Not that you'll be able to compare it to what it once was. Without that benchmark, you'll just notice the smog is worse than from wherever you came (unless you came from Beijing.)

Fog

Every now and again, there's a fog that rolls in. I see it every five years or so. You'll know when it happens because there's plain ol' run-of-the-mill fog and then there's the type of fog that rolls in to Santa Monica.

There was a classic *Three's Company* episode I watched when I was a kid where Jack cannot leave his apartment because of the fog. He opens his front door and this thick pea soup invades the apartment. I laughed because it was ridiculous. I thought fog could never be that dense. Then, I was working in Santa Monica (a few blocks from the Regal Beagle) one night when I walked outside to go home and could not see a thing. The fog is real, my friends.

Marine Layer

If you live near the ocean, you may be surprised to find that your mornings will be overcast. This is what's known as the "marine layer" and will usually blow off before noon.

The point is, you should not bother bringing an umbrella (unless the forecast says there's more than a 60% chance of precipitation) because you'll feel silly carrying it around later. When you select your attire for the day, dress for what it *will be* like in a few hours and not what it is at that time. You'll hate your jeans and fleece jacket once the sun pops through and you're clawing your skin trying to get it to stop sweating.

Earthquakes

. . . or as those who were not subjected to them when growing up call them: "EARTHQUAKE!!!!!!!"

By now, you may have heard that Los Angeles is prone to natural disasters. You may have heard it's built on a potent fault line. You may have heard that potent fault line is not nearly as bad as that other potent fault line it's near. And you may have heard LA is due for "the big one".

Just so you understand what a typical earthquake in Los Angeles entails – there's a little shaking and people will ask those around them, *"Is everyone okay?"* and then they will post on Facebook, *Did anyone just feel that?* or *Did the earth just move?* followed by the quake's seismic reading, location of the epicenter, and that obnoxious meme of the beautiful suburban yard with one lawn chair tipped over and the caption, "We will rebuild".

There are two types of earthquakes: rollers and shakers. The rollers produce a nice rhythmic rolling motion, as if you're on a raft floating on a calm (or turbulent) ocean, while the shakers feel like a very large person fell onto the floor in the apartment above you. That one's more like a boom.

Do NOT run outside when this happens. It is the exact opposite of what to do in the event of a fire and what a sane person trying to preserve their own life would do. You can certainly find a doorway (as you've no doubt been told to) and hope it's not part of a false wall, but rather that it is load-bearing.

Ideally, you find a "triangle of life". To do this, get under a piece of furniture that is up against another piece of furniture so, if it collapses, it will fall at an angle leaving you in a comfy, triangle-shaped pocket filled with some air to breathe.

I was the floor warden at work for several years so I know this will *definitely* work . . . in theory.

Oh, and stay away from windows. Fear not, I've been here two decades and it's never come to that. If it were a problem, the city would not have so many residents, many of whom own multi-million dollar homes perched upon stilts dug into the side of a mountain.

Truth be told, there are earthquakes every day all over the world. If you are worried about them, you can purchase or put together an earthquake kit.

Rain

It does rain in Southern California (do not let Albert Hammond's song *It Rains in Southern California* fool you), but only rarely (January through May, if we're lucky). And when it does, it is either a misting, barely enough to cloud your spectacles, or it's a deluge of biblical proportions (at least it seems to be since the drainage systems are not equipped for actual precipitation).

Even as weather patterns change, rain is still scarce and tends to surprise us. (This explains why a kid was struck by lightning on Venice Beach in 2014. It came on suddenly and no one here ever considers lightning as something that can happen. *Don't they know who we are?! How dare the sky do that to us!*)

Rain is the best thing for Los Angeles. It clears the smog away so you can actually see things in the distance. And the best days for seeing the cityscape is the day after a heavy rain, or even better, a heavy rain on the second day of a long weekend.

Unlike other places, such as the northeast or southeast where a storm causes the humidity to break and then leads to an infestation of mosquitoes, rain here is a boon on all levels for the city . . . except for the mudslides (yet another reason that home on stilts seems like a bad investment).

Mudslides

When it rains intensely after an extended period of little rain, the ground cannot soak up the precipitation fast enough, and so you have mudslides. It changes previously solid earth into a muddy flow. All debris and lots of earth are swept away and into areas they don't belong.

The roads winding through the hills are the most affected when this happens, as is the Pacific Coast Highway.

On a positive note, the natural disaster has inspired the creation of a delicious cocktail mix of vodka, Kahlua, and Bailey's Irish Cream.

Drought

LA used not to get much rain. Recently, it's gotten much less. 2014 brought historic drought conditions and water cutbacks. So far, the change hasn't been noticeable, but given the worsening of climate change and longer periods of drought, the situation threatens to grow worse.

As an aside, you may feel very conflicted between conserving water and keeping your car clean and sparkly for the sake of appearances. Please choose the water. Your car can go a little longer without washes (it's resilient like that), and it's not the worst thing in the world to walk outside and find someone has written "Wash Me" through the dust on your windshield.

One simple technique everyone can employ in order to conserve water is in the shower. First, turn on the water and get wet, then turn it off. You can apply soap and shampoo as thoroughly as you would like. Then turn the water back on for a rinse.

The drought also increases the odds of another natural disaster that upsets Smokey the Bear.

Forest Fires

Unfortunately, for an area that was already severely affected by forest fires, the drought does not help. And given all the national forests in Southern California, Smokey the Bear has his work cut out for him. Most of them occur away from your neck of the woods but, as they get closer, you'll notice it in the air quality and sometimes you'll even get ash or dust your car.

Expect the news to report on a nearby forest fire or two every day during the late summer months. Living near the San Gabriel Mountains, north of Pasadena, and Malibu, put you at a greater risk than, say, Century City or Redondo Beach.

The Desert Air

As you are in the more temperate Southwest, it will surprise you how much you need to drink in order to stay hydrated. But on the flipside, NO HUMIDITY! . . . most of the time.

The Santa Anas

From time to time, the wind will blow dry and hot, but it will BLOW. Oh, will it blow! These are called "the Santa Ana winds" and it knocks everything around, plus gets stuff in your eyes. These are not necessarily winds *from* Santa Ana (about an hour south of downtown, so you know if the winds started there, they would get stuck in traffic on their way up the freeway to Los Angeles). They usually occur between October and March and last only a few days, placing some tree branches on the ground, but nothing too traumatic.

El Niño

Every two to seven years, "El Niño" will kick in and give us crazy storms to the point you start researching ark rentals. This actually represents a welcome respite from the same ol', same ol'. It's when warm water in the Pacific replaces the cooler surface water and messes with the climate. When that warmer water shifts eastward, atmospheric moisture follows along with prolonged droughts and other extreme weather, and lasts around nine months to two years.

Then, it is frequently followed by another phenomena called "La Niña" which typically produces below-average rainfall (as if that were possible) here in the Southwest.

Friendly Visitors

The low humidity and characteristics of the ecosystem do decrease the volume of mosquitoes, but bring plenty of gnats, silverfish, ants, termites, fruit flies, black widow spiders, squirrels, raccoons, and cockroaches – giant reddish-orange ones that freak the hell out of you because they can fly, and then the small brown ones that annoy the hell out of you because they're disgusting, along with harmless snakes, and rattlesnakes. (If a snake hisses at you, that's not one of the harmless ones.)

You will also see coyotes and mountain lions in the hills, some bears invading neighborhoods and, by the beaches, dolphins like to swim. Sharks rarely make their way over, unless there's an open call for *Sharknado 4* (coming soon to a theater near you).

Oh, and they also say that LA is #2 in the nation in terms of rat population, but I've never seen one here . . . unless we're counting agents. (Zing!)

FREEWAYS

The higher speed roadways are not called highways or thruways here for they are (mostly) non-toll roads. And whereas you may have grown used to referring to these interstates and main thoroughfares using the prefixes "route" or "I", as in "Route 140" or "I-95," you will now precede all roadway numbers with the word "the". You will drive on "THE 5" or "THE 134" and all will resemble a parking lot for the majority of your waking hours.

You may know how freeways and highways have been designed. During the Eisenhower Administration, highways were put in place with a straight-forward numerical system; north-south were given odd numbers and east-west were given even.

That's exactly how the 101 is . . . until it isn't. The 101 has two directions, north/south which is logical given its number, but after you go through Hollywood and over the hill, it veers to the left, or west. (Remember, I said the coastline is not always north/south.) So you may be on the 101 North with the sun directly in your face at sundown. It does not mean the earth has shifted.

One thing that doesn't help is that many exits do not say the direction you will be going in, but rather a city you are headed toward. Going north on the 405, you will come upon the 10 where the sign will ask you if you'd like to go to Santa Monica or Los Angeles and you'll say to yourself, *"But I thought Santa Monica WAS Los Angeles."* Oh, sure, you'll quickly realize you can't get any more west than Santa Monica without a dinghy, but before you've gotten your bearings, the signage is posted to test your existing knowledge of the city and not as a guide for newbies.

Oh, and some freeways (I'm looking at you, 5 South!) have a connector to the 10 going east, but not west. You can get onto the 5 from both directions off the 10, but can't connect this way. It's always nice to find this out as you're passing the road you wanted to take and are now bound for Anaheim. (To avoid this, take the 5 S to the 110 S and then you'll have the 10 W connector available to you.)

GPS, Waze, Mapquest, Google Maps, and whichever traffic app is your favorite will be your best friend. This is not a city where you can simply take the next exit, circle underneath the highway, and pop back onto it heading in the opposite direction.

On-ramps can be tricky too. For all the square footage that LA covers, there is very little room for many freeway on-ramps. Sometimes you'll have twenty feet during which to punch your Prius up to 60 miles per hour before you're knocked off the road by an Escalade driven by a someone who can barely see over the steering wheel.

Similarly, you should be wary that many exits force you to slam on your brakes in order to keep from slamming into the bend. You may need to decelerate from 60 to 25 in only a few feet.

In the advanced class, you'll learn not to take Highland onto the 101 if you intend to exit at Barham (the "Barham Shuffle" as my friend calls it) which requires you to dart over 5 lanes of heavy traffic in less than a mile. (You should take Cahuenga instead.) And that you need to get in the left lane *but* slow down in order to take the 90-degree turn from the 110 N to the 5 N.

STYLE OF DRESS

Creative types and production people need to feel comfortable as do surfers and street urchins. This constitutes the majority of town. Writers dress down (and many, quite frankly, don't know *how* to dress up); beachgoers may not own a pair of shoes outside their flip-flops; most execs just go pants and shirt (tie optional); and actors do whatever they need to in order to perpetuate their images.

Unbutton that top button and lose that tie. Replace those wing tips with loafers or go all the way with sandals. People in LA dress more laid back. But if you're an agent or a studio executive, you will most definitely be dressed sharply. It's your uniform. Otherwise, you can prepare to dress down. And for heaven's sake, UNTUCK your shirt! Oh, and if you do go with a tie, then you will not be able to leave the top two buttons open on your linen shirt. (It's not complete anarchy here, after all.)

On average, you'll see far more suits downtown than you will in the rest of Los Angeles County combined. Typically, Sunday attire is worn everywhere.

For the ladies, the same goes for business suits. If you do not need one for your job, then dress for comfort, but nothing too revealing, unless you are selling a project to a studio executive or trying to get an agent, in which case you should by all means dress as revealingly as possible. (I kid, I kid.)

And ladies, if you are going to the Hollywood night clubs, the stiletto pumps are required. If not, flip-flops are fine. Yes, for you too.

The person wearing a suit always stands out in a job interview, and not in a "head and shoulders above the rest" way, but an "oh, look at the newbie" way.

But the town does love a good dress-up night or two. Suits will be required for one of the many soirées from award presentations to red carpet events like movie premieres, so do have such dress up fare ready to go. It's not so much *what* you are wearing as it is *who* you are wearing.

DEMEANOR

This style of dress is an indicator of demeanor.

Laid Back

A Southern Californian is, by nature, easy-going. Relax, bro. Chill out. This is really a misnomer. Natives, yes, but most industry professionals are constantly stressed. But they do it in an open-collared shirts so it seems as if they're laid back. There are so many people from other places that you won't register the stereotype unless you're near the beach.

Most people will not sound like the *Saturday Night Live* sketch *The Californians*. Guys might call you "bro" or "brah", but "dude" is the predominant word used.

Girls might end statements with question marks and use the word "like" a lot. A LOT. And there are one-syllable words that inexplicably get turned into two-syllable words. For example, simple words like "try" or "bring" become "tuh-rye" and "buh-ring" as in *He, like, came to my, like, birthday party, and like, did not buh-ring anything?*

Why the laidback personality? Because they *can* be. Anywhere else across the country people need to have contingency plans — *Okay, I'll need to bring a coat in case of rain, or have something to do indoors if my golf game is canceled.* Or *What if bad weather changes my travel plans?* In Los Angeles, it's simply, *I'm doing this tomorrow and nothing will prevent me from that.* There's usually no contemplation needed.

Most days are exactly as they expect it to be, free of conflict.

Friendliness

LA residents can be very friendly. The sun is shining and it leads to smiles on their faces. Plus, you never know who is going to be your ally during this, one of the great struggles of your life. People talk, they introduce themselves, they make plans to keep in touch but you'll also find a large segment of the population that has their shields up because you never know what type of crazy is out there and it's better to keep your distance.

This is not only a Los Angeles thing. Someone once told me of a study that said 50,000 is the largest number of people that can be in a community before it becomes too large for you to relate to. That means that in a city of nine million, your village instincts shut down. You become disconnected from individuals that so much of your day is spent with your head down and eyes straight ahead.

This makes things awkward when passing people on the sidewalk. You're all alone, walking down a side street when a stranger walks towards you. All it takes is a simple grunt, a slight nod of the head, or anything to acknowledge the other person. But you enter the other person's space and think, *Do I look down? Do I stare straight ahead? Just don't make eye contact.* Is it really too much to look at them?

In fact, it becomes so rare that when someone actually gives a glint of acknowledgement, it might shock you. I have had people say, "*Hey*" as they passed with such a kindliness that I have wanted to follow that person and compliment them on doing so. (Of course, maybe that's why nobody does it, for fear that they'll ingratiate themselves to strangers and be stuck with a stalker.)

You'll form your own unique opinions on friendliness. You may get back what you put in.

Flakiness

It's easy to make plans, but following through takes effort and commitment. (Ugh!) The easy-going demeanor in Los Angeles has a down side, and that is that people tend to flake a lot, because, well, whatever, man. Making concrete plans won't be as concrete to them as they are to you. You Midwesterners who say what you mean and follow through on your promises may be taken aback the most. We'll speak of this more later in the book.

Sense of Entitlement

Yes, it sounds mean, but ask around; you will find the first thing many people observe in this town is a sense of entitlement. More so than in the town from where you're coming, a percentage of Los Angeles residents feel it is their

God-given right to do whatever they want, ignorant of any effects their actions may have. You see it in their driving, in their self-important way of holding themselves, in their seemingly oblivious glares.

This is LA, after all: Home of the Beautiful People. No one can be that beautiful and expected to remain on the same level as you lesser people. You'll shake your head and wonder how someone can be so disinterested in living by the simple rules of a society.

One case in point happened at the LA Marathon where I had positioned myself along the sidelines near Mile 22 (that point where most runners lament every previous life decision) in order to support a friend who was running.

This woman, carrying a baby stroller, decides that *this* is a good place to cross the street. Instead of waiting for the pack of runners to dissipate enough so she could get through easily, she just plowed forward onto the course, without even considering to pause, as if she were making a beeline to the restroom in a stadium concourse.

In her effort to avoid these athletes, she caused them to sidestep her (not easy at Mile 22), bumped into a couple, spun into a couple others, and also caused them to bump into each other in their efforts to avoid her. When she reached the other side, and it was explained to her in no uncertain terms by a concerned onlooker how rude and disrespectful she was to the people sacrificing their bodies out there, this woman simply smiled and said, "Gee, you're so nice," and kept walking, leaving shaken runners in her wake trying to regain their momentum as their bodies began to shut down.

This was Brentwood, which you'll find has a higher ratio of these incidents, but it's merely one example of a prevalent attitude you'll find.

Healthiness

Los Angeles is one of the leading communities nationwide for health and fitness. Bike lanes, vegan restaurants, farmer's markets, outdoor boot camp workouts, beach yoga classes, pilates studios, yogilates, spinning and kickboxing classes, juice bars — oh, Lord the juice bars — permeate the landscape.

Los Angeles is a hub of healthy living. It is not, ironically, the "fittest" city, probably because of the hours and hours people spend in their cars or on the set of a commercial production shoot that is slated to air only in a remote region of West Virginia subsisting on a steady diet of salty pretzels and Red Vines licorice.

Spirituality

Someone, at some point, will provide you (unsolicited, mind you) with your astrological chart. They will ask you where you were born and the exact time and date, and then will give you a ten-page document that is surprisingly accurate about who you are. It will also tell you stuff like your sun sign and what will happen to you or who you will become later in life or in your *next* life. . . or next Thursday, whenever. Just go with it. Thank them for taking the time to do it and never look at it again.

If you are of a religious belief, you will have your pick of the litter here. You could probably find a group of fellow practitioners with whom to convene. This includes Scientology which has a huge center in Hollywood and is always accepting new members. They've hit a bit of a valley in terms of popularity due to former members speaking out against them, but if you're looking for a religion that could help your career, they are always open to new members.

For simple peace and relaxation, Los Angeles has some very spiritual venues including the Church of Self-Realization in the Palisades where some of Mahatma Gandhi's ashes are interred, and the Peace Awareness Labyrinth on Adams.

CUISINE

No one cuisine stands out as the thing LA is known for like, say, the seafood in Boston, the BBQ in Texas, the deep dish pizza in Chicago, or the heart attack waiting to happen in New Orleans. You can get anything you want here . . . except good Chinese food or pizza.

A-ha! That is what we *used to* say. Now there *are* places for good Chinese food and pizza. They may not be right outside your door like in New York City, but you can find them.

You can get authentic Chinese food in Monterey Park or San Gabriel. The menus are in Chinese and you can get great Dim Sum. Chinatown is an option as well.

As for pizza, there are many more chains now that serve more than adequate pizza. Still more provide that New York City atmosphere, where they make the pies ahead of time with toppings on them and display them for you to choose a slice of this, a slice of that.

Of course, if you like sushi, you'll have many high-quality places to choose from. And gourmet burger joints are all the rage. For seafood, these places may not be as good as San Francisco or Seattle, but that's a matter of opinion. For what you're going for, yes, it's quite good.

There's also a Thaitown, a Little Tokyo, a Koreatown, a Persian district in Westwood, Indian places, Ethiopian spots, and so many Mexican places that you'll find certain streets paved with fresh salsa and/or guacamole.

Los Angeles does have such popular staples you could not find elsewhere such as In n' Out Burger, Fatburger, Tommy's Burger, Carl Jr's, Jack in the Box, taco stands, hot dog stands like Pink's, and French dip locales such as Philippe's.

Don't even get me started on the food truck scene. What's your favorite cuisine? It's a safe bet there's a darned good food truck serving it. In fact, the best cheesesteak in town is not at a brick and mortar spot, but a popular food truck: South Philly Experience.

And, as this is a major city, you can always count on a Starbucks being nearby, probably next to a Chipotle, which is down the street from another Starbucks next to another Chipotle.

Overall, you may not find that comfort food you got on a daily basis back home, like a White Castle or Waffle House, but open your mind to new frontiers. Trust me, you'll eat well.

POLITICAL VIEWS

LA is liberal. Okay, maybe not as liberal as San Francisco or Austin, Texas, because most inhabitants don't want to rock the boat and have anything more to worry about than why their agent hasn't called back, but since the whole town pretty much flies in the face of conservative beliefs, what with its drive for sustainability in farming and non-GMO foods through an abundance of farmer's markets, legitimate concern for climate change, a large LGBT community, an even larger Hispanic community, and, most notably, the Fox News chestnut that "Hollywood movies are ruining the fabric of society", it could seem pretty liberal. (Not exactly a conservative Utopia.)

The biggest liberals are the famous ones who host top politicians who gum up traffic for half a day.

There are conservatives sprinkled throughout, but they won't gain much traction. Viewing parties for elections is more than likely to happen at the home of a Democrat, with only the occasional outlier here and there.

But it's a free country and you will not be kicked out for your political views. That being said, it pays to remain low-key as you never know who your boss will be and the best way to endear yourself to him/her. Early in your career, your outspoken politics should take a back seat to the politics of Hollywood.

SPORTS FANDOM

What other city has so many teams to choose from (and yet has lost not one, but *two* NFL franchises)?

Los Angeles Dodgers

Holding the heart of most Los Angelenos are the Dodgers, or as they are frequently called, *Los Doyers*. Fans bleed Dodger blue and hate the San Francisco Giants. They arrive to Dodger Stadium late and leave early, but do not hold that against them as the place is very difficult to get to. Set in the hills referred to as Chavez Ravine and isolated from the noise and commotion of the city, it is a little slice of heaven.

Vin Scully, the greatest sports announcer of all time, is a patron saint of Los Angeles. He is special. No one speaks ill of him, and nor should they.

Los Angeles Angels

About 45 minutes south of the city (without traffic), reside the Los Angeles (formerly the California and then Anaheim) Angels. They are officially in Anaheim which is officially in Orange County and not many of you without a connection to Orange County will bother rooting for them. Besides, if you work in Los Angeles, it's nearly impossible to get down there in time to see the first pitch. At least, being late to Dodger Stadium still gets you home relatively soon after the game whereas, in Anaheim, you have to drive that same 45 minutes (without traffic) before you're finally home. On a school night? Nah.

Los Angeles Lakers

First and foremost, Los Angeles is a Lakers town. Many will say the Dodgers trump the Lakers in terms of popularity, because fans of the "purple and gold" have the "fair weather" label and it's not unjustified. Of course, they'll vehemently refute this, but it won't change things. Dodgers fans are much more steady.

When the team is doing well, i.e. passes the second round of the playoffs, you will see Lakers flags pop up on cars. Though even when they win, it's not like other cities where every bar is packed and the energy is palpable.

In fairness, Los Angelenos have so many other things available to them that when one thing doesn't hold their interests, they can find something else that will.

Los Angeles Clippers

Then, there are the Clippers, LA's perennial doormat, who have recently turned the corner. The Clippers and their fans are fast becoming en vogue and the bandwagon is happily accepting applications. When you develop your aversion to Lakers fans, you'll find Clippers fans are much more acceptable.

Los Angeles Kings

The Kings are there too. They have a small, but rabid fan base. Even with their recent successes, their parades have not garnered the typical Championship Parade turnout, but there may not be a better evening of sports entertainment in Los Angeles than going downtown to see the Kings play live.

Los Angeles Galaxy

And there's a soccer team, too! They are located in Carson. No one knows where that is, but a little cursory research will reveal it's south of Los Angeles, about 30 minutes away (without traffic).

Los Angeles WNBA entry

Finally, it's hard to forget about the WNBA participant. This is mainly because no one knew about it in the first place. (They are called the Sparks.)

Other Sports

Beach volleyball tournaments down in the South Bay also gather a lot of attention. Muscle Beach bodybuilding competitions are held regularly in Venice. Long Beach transforms a strip of road into a Grand Prix once a year. The Derby Dolls are also an underground treat if you enjoy watching tough chicks on wheels push each other around in the sport of roller derby. (And the status on an NFL franchise is soon to change . . . maybe.)

TOURISM

LA is a popular tourist destination. There's an entire cottage industry for visitors set up. It's possible your career in Los Angeles even started during a school field trip when you decided to stay. Of course, once you become a local, your goal will be to avoid these tourists at all costs. That means staying away from Hollywood Boulevard and the strand at Venice and Santa Monica beaches, for starters. Rodeo Drive attracts a lot of tourists as well, but they're actually kind of a welcome change from the snooty, plastic surgery-laden residents of Beverly Hills.

Of course, they spend much of their time at the studios and theme parks, so you'll also want to avoid those too.

EAST V. WEST

If you're arriving in Southern California from the East Coast, you will be in for quite a shock. Not only are you now behind the rest of the country by hours, but the ocean is ON THE WRONG SIDE.

Using the ocean as a marker may confuse you at first. Prepare to spend a lot of time going *east* to get to the ocean, which will put you in downtown Los Angeles and further away from any of the beach cities. You will outgrow this, though it may take a while as you kick yourself for not thinking it through.

Another thing to which you will not be accustomed is the sprawl. The East Coast crams its cities next to one another. It's as if they were conceived with horse and carriage transportation in mind, whereas the West Coast is one expansive territory with large areas of land between major metropolises. You can go hours on the highway between major cities. San Francisco, Vegas, and San Diego are the nearest ones and you'll wonder if they only popped up because someone got tired of driving and had to find a bathroom.

A third prominent difference between the two coasts is the conflicting attitude. New Yorkers complain about Los Angeles natives (*They're too laid back!*) and the natives complain about New Yorkers (*They're too intense* and *If they don't like it, why don't they just move back?*) Yet they all somehow coexist.

CONCLUSION

That's pretty much your introduction to the region -- "Los Angeles, please meet [insert your name here]; [insert your name here], this is Los Angeles."

This chapter gets all that first date stuff out of the way. *So how long have you been a city? What do you have for fun around here?* It's like when you visit a foreign land and have three or four phrases under your belt so you don't look too green.

Now you two cuckoo kids spend some time getting to know one another.

CHAPTER 2 - BEFORE YOU MOVE

INTRO

Wherever you go, it's very hard to leave a place you're familiar with and set up a new life for yourself, but moving to Los Angeles is especially difficult. Expect a transitional period where everything comes at you in one chunk: how to behave, career advice, where to go, and when to leave your place in order to get there in time – all for the purpose of beginning your new life and settling in for the long haul.

This period may feel like a honeymoon – new places to party, everything is exciting and new, just like love (as stated in the theme from *The Love Boat*). The more people you know, the more places you begin to like and the more customs you become acclimatized to, the more you'll feel at home.

Hollywood can feel like one big extended college education, where your schedule fluctuates and you have freedom. Being among so many creative people can inspire you and the never-ending sunlight can make you feel alive. Eventually, you'll settle into a routine and have to get down to business.

BE PREPARED

Like any move, you can do things ahead of time to prepare yourself for your new life, and that means secure some leads on jobs, a residence, and a social group.

Many times, one leads to another. If you have a roommate all set up, then you have someone to hang out with. Perhaps that roommate will also provide you with a lead on a job.

Announce Your Intentions

Tell everyone you know — your hairdresser, professor, ex-partner (with whom you're still on good terms), your great aunt's creepy stepson — that you're moving to Los Angeles. Put those feelers out there. You'll be surprised who will have information that could be useful and how anxious people will be to help you and support this bold move you're making.

Utilize every name you can in order to gain that experience. I had a cousin I'd never met who knew this guy. At her request, I called him for my internship. Since no one expects your resume to blow them away at the early stages of your adult life, then just knowing someone is the way to go. This includes people you may not officially know.

Alumni Clubs

If you went to a large college, check your alumni list. More than likely, you will learn of a few alumni that have come to Los Angeles and perhaps even become successful (but not too successful, otherwise, they might not have time for you). If you have an alumni office in Los Angeles, as many schools do, you might want to contact them.

Many colleges even have a bar that caters to your alumni fanbase; that is, the bigger schools. It would behoove you to find out which bar it is and make it a point to watch a game there upon first arriving.

Will Work for Food

If you can have a job set up through any of these connections or on your own, that's a bonus, more weight off your shoulders. Any job will do to start, as that would just be to pay the bills, but if you happen to have something that provides you with a step toward your goal, even better.

If you are not immediately in dire straits where you need money to eat, maybe you can set up an unpaid internship. Unpaid positions were invented here in Los Angeles. The thinking is, there are tons of people who are willing to work for free just to gain experience (and make connections), even if it's a thankless job that any monkey can do like lowly production assistant or NBC Comedy Development Executive.

Definitely start thinking like a creative before you arrive. Have a reel if you're an actor, some experience if you're an editor, a script if you're a writer, etc. It'll give you a step up right at the get go. (Others will catch up, but there's so much sensory overload that having some things taken care of early on will set you more at ease).

A ROOF OVER YOUR HEAD

LA is the most transitive place in the country. Couches are used as addresses almost as much as houses and condos. Knowing where you will come home to on a regular basis is helpful, but living out of a suitcase in the beginning is not the worst thing in the world.

Once in town, you can pick a day to canvass the area you're partial to and start calling on "For Rent" signs. LA is nothing if not transitional. There's always an influx and an exodus, so it provides a slew of housing opportunities. Many people are comfortable renting a place without first seeing it in person. Should you rather just do your legwork online, here are the sites most people use:

- www.westsiderentals.com
- www.craigslist.com
- www.roommates.com

One thing you should know is, though Los Angeles covers miles, each neighborhood provides a different flavor, a different lure. One block can have a very different personality from the next. Take the corner of Bundy and Wilshire, where Santa Monica, Brentwood, and West Los Angeles all converge, for instance. The residents of all three possess different traits and each area comes with a slightly different vibe.

Sometimes your residential choices, especially early on, are limited due to monetary concerns where you'll need to rent a pad with no kitchen deep in the valley, where rents are cheap, or you'll be the fifth roommate in a three-bedroom apartment in Koreatown. But if you can afford any place that will fit your personality and interests then, by all means, spread a wide net.

You'll also be presented with questions like:

- Hardwood floors or carpeting?
- Air-conditioning or ceiling fans?
- Gated parking or carport?
- Old-style charm or modern convenience?

Neither one nor the other represents a clear choice; but each has pros and cons. For example, if hardwood floors are your thing, you'll hear every little thing your upstairs or downstairs neighbor does. And if it's carpeting that you seek, prepare to vacuum more than you think is necessary in order to keep it clean. It's totally your preference. This is why every type of home is occupied.

In a perfect world, you'll live near your job in a neighborhood you really like and in an ideal residence.

When given the choice, how do you know which area will be best for you? Here's a description of many of the little nooks and crannies of the city:

Abbot Kinney

It's a street in Venice with shops and restaurants. Now currently attracting beach types and young, trendy folks. "First Fridays" are popular as food trucks populate the area and shops stay open late for customers to meander up and down the street on the first Friday of every month.

Atwater Village

Just on the flip side of the 5 from Los Feliz, the village has gotten younger, hipper, and cooler over the past few years thanks to an influx of bearded hipsters. Much of this is due to the fact there are nine bars within a mile-long stretch of Los Feliz Boulevard and a nightly taco truck.

Baldwin Hills

A peaceful, residential area along one of the main roads to the airport (La Brea) that no one really knows about as it's hidden in the hills. If asked where you live, be prepared to say it twice when people reply with, *Huh? Where's that?* because no one turns their heads to the left or right when they're stuck in traffic on their way to the airport.

Beverly/Fairfax to Beverly/La Brea and Robertson/Pico

These are two locations that are located in densely packed neighborhoods along main roads. Each features a large Jewish population who will take to the streets on foot every Sabbath. These areas are where you go for your Kosher foods and good authentic delis.

Beverly Hills

It's all that you've seen in the movies – shop girls work on commission (*Pretty Woman*), the police force dresses and acts like Judge Reinhold (*Beverly Hills Cop*), and Dylan and Kelly are constantly breaking up and getting back together. (I've never seen one episode of *Beverly Hills, 90210*, clearly.) There are basically three sections: the hills (huge, ridiculously priced celebrity houses), downtown (Rodeo Drive), and the slums (apartments, duplexes, and ridiculously priced regular person houses).

Meanwhile, Beverly Hills-adjacent is the area just *outside* Beverly Hills, named so just to appeal to people who can't quite afford the real thing. It's like calling New Jersey "Upper West side-adjacent."

Brentwood

This is an interesting area on the Westside (west of the 405). The personality of residents is one focused on appearances and possessions, but the demographics are mainly split in two – wealthy families and post-college grads who want to *become* wealthy families.

Real estate prices are among the highest in the city along the northern side, but there are also plenty of apartments in what are referred to as either the "Brenthood" or the "Slums of Brentwood."

The entitlement vibe is more prevalent here, so if your kids are spoiled brats, this would be the school district to send them.

Burbank

The furthest north you can go before anyone asks, *You live where?* It's lovely, beautiful, safe, but not rent-controlled. Still, it has whatever you seek in terms of entertainment with plenty of restaurants, shops, theaters, and an Ikea.

Burbank houses a good portion of the studios and networks in town including NBC, ABC, Warner Brothers, and Disney, with Universal just a couple of miles down the road. If you envision yourself working in the industry, you'd be playing your odds by living here.

(That said, if you play your odds and move to Burbank, but end up working at Twentieth Century Fox, you're not going to like your commute.)

Century City

As Universal City was conceived as a backlot for Universal Studios, Century City is the area behind Twentieth Century Fox. Really it's just a small area along Santa Monica Boulevard between West LA and Beverly Hills that features the Century City Mall (a.k.a. Westfield Century City). Oh, and if you were wondering where Bruce Willis rescued all those hostages from Hans Gruber in Die Hard, the Nakatomi Towers are right behind the mall.

Culver City

Formerly a place where you would feel as if you'd stepped back in time, it has gotten a much-needed makeover in its bustling downtown area. Property values are up and it's become a destination city with subway access, condominiums, shops and restaurants.

It's quite the historic area too, thanks to the late studio mogul Harry Culver. His creation is now Sony Studios but the ghosts of such movie classics as *Gone with the Wind* and *The Wizard of Oz* are still there.

On a side note, Culver City is its own incorporated city so, although it's right smack dab in the middle of the city of Los Angeles, you cannot participate in LA's mayoral elections. The good news is, public services, such as trash pickup, are excellent.

Downtown LA (DTLA)

Thanks to a huge urban revitalization project, downtown LA now feels like a *real* city! Loft apartments and the energetic LA Live entertainment venue highlight the new charm. Though it is still a transitioning district, with homeless and nouveau riche in equal measure.

The question has always been, *Why would anyone live downtown?* If you don't work there, you'll have to leave downtown in order to get to work. You can do it by METRO to some places, but for real freedom of access, you'll need a car. And why live in the middle of a real city if you have a car? It kind of defeats the purpose.

This is also where Chinatown is and also Union Station, the center of our public transportation universe.

Eagle Rock/Highland Park/Mt. Washington

This is truly an oasis in the city as you're nestled among hills just northeast of central Los Angeles, disconnected from the urban landscape. I'm told there's also a friendly vibe where people say "Good morning!" and wave as they pass each other.

The conglomerate of neighborhoods possesses more of a distinctive character than other areas and is becoming the new hipster-ville. It's Silverlake for those who can't afford it. In fact, Highland Park was written up in *LA Weekly* as LA's greatest neighborhood. There's also plenty of wildlife, including coyotes, hawks, and undomesticated parrots (trying to make it in Hollywood).

The area also has easy access to four major freeways – the 5, the 110, the 134, and the 2 (assuming you consider the 2 a "major freeway"). That's particularly noteworthy since I've been on all those freeways and never once exited into any of them.

Echo Park/Elysian Park/Elysian Heights

Along the northern perimeter of central Los Angeles (i.e. downtown), you'll come upon these areas, with a surprisingly non-urban feel to them. They're up in the hills with parks and a lake and a nice vista of the surrounding neighborhoods below.

These areas have easy access to downtown, Pasadena, and contain Dodgers Stadium.

El Segundo

Are you in the airline industry? If not, why would you want to live in El Segundo? Though it is near Manhattan Beach (and the ocean, obviously), which is nice, and a friend has referred to it as "Mayberry by the Sea". But mainly, you can roll out of bed and you're at your airline gate. Did I mention it's near the airport?

Glendale

Little Armenia is in the Los Feliz vicinity. This is *Big* Armenia. In fact, they might as well call it "Armenia". It's become a destination city recently with great shops and restaurants highlighted by the Americana Mall which is the Glendale version of The Grove (which we will discuss in a moment).

And then there's the part of town that's not so nice, but why focus on that?

Hancock Park/Larchmont

You may never know that you're in the Hancock Park area, but for one popular street of shops and restaurants located between Melrose and Third Street called Larchmont. In fact, I'd feel comfortable saying that Larchmont is the "Abbot Kinney of Hancock Park."

The area has some charm and many expensive, older houses. As a whole, it features all types from families to young professionals to the college students coming over from nearby LA City College.

Hollywood

The pros of living in Hollywood: mass transportation, its central location (20 minutes from wherever you need to go, barring traffic, of course), and cheaper rent. Cons: everything else.

It's not like you see in postcards. It's a testament to Hollywood (the industry) and their ability to transform a dirty, rundown area that is Hollywood (the district) into what you see in postcards and on TV. Consisting of older buildings and congested roads, it is a practical and functional option for many. And if you don't mind helicopters overhead, you'll enjoy the convenience of living in H-Town. (P.S. No one calls it that.)

Holmby Hills

If you can afford a home in Holmby Hills, you don't need this book.

Inglewood

Next on the docket for gentrification, Inglewood is shedding its reputation as a dangerous place you wouldn't want to be after dark. It's near the airport and so deserves a chance to show us what it can do.

Koreatown

Are you Korean? Do you like Korean food and/or karaoke? It's cheap here, next to downtown, and along the 101 freeway which brings you into Hollywood and the valley easily.

Little Armenia

It's next to Los Feliz and you'll find a lot of Armenians here, at least those that didn't want to live in Glendale.

Little Filipino Town

It's next to downtown and I didn't know it existed until this past year. But then, I'm not Filipino.

Little Italy

Ha! Totally kidding. There's no Little Italy. (You should see the look on your face.) It's like telling the high school freshmen that the science wing is just past the swimming pool when there's no swimming pool . . . and no science wing. (It *is* a religious-based high school, after all.)

Little Tokyo

A small part of downtown LA where you can find great ramen and sushi places. An even smaller area dedicated to these shops and restaurants lies on the west side and is called "*Sawtelle Japantown*". (I've also heard it referred to as "*Little Osaka*".) This two block stretch on Sawtelle just north of Olympic features about a half dozen curry and ramen places for those who can't get to Little Tokyo.

Long Beach

The LBC represents the southernmost point of Los Angeles County and, if you take out Los Angeles, San Francisco, and San Diego, Long Beach is the fourth-largest city (seventh overall for those in remedial math) in California!

By itself, there are lots of perks to living there, such as the
Belmont Shore area and downtown Long Beach which
features such popular attractions as the Aquarium of the
Pacific, Queen Mary, and annual Long Beach Grand Prix. It is
a charter city and thus governed by its own charter document
instead of state, regional, or national laws.

That little tidbit aside, if you are going to be working in
the industry, it will be a grind traveling to and from.

Los Feliz

Do you want a New York feel to your life without the
New York attitude or climate? Then quaint Los Feliz may be
your best choice. The high rent and diversity of food options
also give it as much of a New York feel as you are able to get
out here. It also has a walkability factor.

Plus, it's nestled at the base of Griffith Park which
features the Greek Theatre, hiking grounds, a golf course,
horseback riding, a zoo, an observatory, and the best view of
the Hollywood sign you'll get. You'll also see more trees here
than anywhere else in the city.

Malibu

Malibu is what you would imagine - an upscale community
with surfers, college students (Pepperdine), and celebrities. It's
far enough away from the city and just up the coast from
Santa Monica to feel removed from the rigmarole . . . (though
you will *remain* removed from Santa Monica should there be a
mudslide on the Pacific Coast Highway).

Marina del Rey

Do you sail? Are you an avid stand-up paddle boarder? Do
you like the beach, but want something more upscale than the
Venice scene? Ta Da! Here's your new home! An ocean
community, it is tucked along a marina (go figure) adjacent to
Venice and Playa del Rey.

Your main roadways will be Lincoln Boulevard,
Washington Boulevard, and the seldom-used 91 Freeway
which will bring you swiftly to the *over*used 405 Freeway.

Miracle Mile

Not really a miracle, it's a stretch of real estate on Wilshire between La Brea and Fairfax that features the Los Angeles County Museum of Art (LACMA) and the La Brea Tarpits. Outside of those LA exclusives, there are three Starbucks and one Coffee Bean along that stretch.

It is littered with lots of old-style Hollywood duplexes with high ceilings and hardwood floors that represent as much charm and personality in an abode as we can offer. Parking restrictions aren't as bad as other places in the city and you have easy access to The Grove. If you'd like to go anywhere else, you'll be in traffic just to get to the corner of your block.

North Hollywood

It's not connected to Hollywood, though it is North – as in "over the hill" north. It's cheaper and you'll have access to everything the valley has to offer. The last line along METRO's red line stops there, so if you really insist on riding it, here's another residential option for you. Like Burbank, anything north of this locale falls into the category of "Where the hell is that?!"

Pacific Palisades

A slice of heaven along the ocean. It's not Malibu, and it's not Brentwood, but does, in fact, have the best elements of both, and provides a peaceful community. You can get there via Sunset which doesn't start backing up until closer to Bundy, so you'll be able to open 'er up and inhale some ocean air as you drive along the winding road before you meet traffic, which is refreshing.

The ocean is minutes away and there are plenty of shops and restaurants in the small stretch of commercial area in town so you don't have to leave the neighborhood on the weekends if that's your desire.

Palms/Mar Vista

It's been called "the armpit of the 405 and 10 freeways". Hey, that means it's easy access to them. Because of this, it's more expensive than you would imagine, yet features nice residential areas tucked in there, while still requiring only a short trip to the ocean.

Pasadena/South Pasadena

The original "nice", it was really the first suburb outside of downtown Los Angeles and has kept up its reputation as a place that has everything. It's charming, filled with old mansions, and kept so tidy because it has a tradition of being filmed at least once a year during the Rose Bowl Parade. It does contain the Rose Bowl where you can experience a huge flea market every Sunday along with exciting games during football season, and the California Institute of Technology (a.k.a. Cal Tech).

Of course, it is along the easternmost border of anyplace you'll ever need to go so plan ahead whenever leaving for an appointment . . . or a visit to a friend's . . . or anytime you just need to leave Pasadena.

South Pasadena isn't as much of a draw as Pasadena but is provides a gateway for a quicker commute into the city.

Playa del Rey/Playa Vista

Formerly *just* a beach community, it is now "Silicon BEACH" as Google is building a huge facility inside the town's borders. Buy property there now. And if you do live there, it's got access to the beaches, close proximity to Loyola Marymount College and LAX, and some quaint neighborhoods that are off the beaten path.

Santa Monica

Another city not under the rule of the city of Los Angeles, Santa Monica is sometimes referred to as "the Home of the Homeless". (And why wouldn't you choose to live here if you didn't live anywhere?) It is the only beach city I have ever experienced that doesn't feel like a beach city until you're *literally on* the beach. Two blocks away, you would be just as comfortable wearing loafers and carrying a briefcase.

The city is basically split into thirds. The northern most third is where the wealthiest people live as it is tucked neatly among Brentwood, Malibu, and Pacific Palisades and contains the Santa Monica Mountains.

Then there's the more tightly congested major streets and commercial districts featuring popular outdoor shopping venue Third Street Promenade between Wilshire and Broadway. It will become more tightly congested as the light rail begins operation in 2016.

Finally, there's the lowermost third which is the beach version of Hollywood with helicopters going over head, lower income housing, and a seedier feel. If there's going to be a murder, odds are that it will happen here. Having said that, Main Street does offer some nice dining and socializing options.

Down here is where you'll find it gets *beachier*. More flip flops, more surfboards.

Silverlake

Though it is next to Los Feliz, I have been scolded for combining the two when discussing each, though only by those living in Los Feliz as Silverlake is the hipster center of the universe and they wouldn't care what I said about it.

There *is* a very pretty lake there (though the name of it escapes me) and, as a bonus, it comes with TWO dog parks. The one thing that always bugs me is that the streets are not laid out in a grid system and I will inevitably get lost *every single time* I find myself there.

South Bay

This area consists of Manhattan Beach, Hermosa Beach, Redondo Beach, and even the tucked away enclave known as Palos Verdes. Love Hollywood, but never, EVER want to go there? This is the place for you.

It's along the ocean, but oddly, the farther south you go, it is nowhere NEAR the highway as the 405 makes a sudden cut toward the east, so once you're in Redondo Beach, you're miles away from escape. That's a good thing as it keeps the masses from invading the area. But if you ever have to go anywhere, plan your day accordingly. And don't even think about heading up to Hollywood on a Friday. If you do, it might be quicker to bike. And that's like 15 miles. Seriously.

Hermosa Beach is a bastion of suspended adolescence for the recent college graduates who spend many a night on the

Hermosa Beach Strand, a strip of bars and restaurants, reliving their debauchery days.

As for Manhattan Beach, what more can be said of a beach town that charges a cover?

South Central

It's the home of the University of Southern California. You may someday run/walk a 5K that ends in the Coliseum.

Thai Town

Hollywood Boulevard between Normandie and Western, along the more eastern end of Hollywood, you can find Thai restaurants here, as you can throughout the rest of Los Angeles. You won't really notice that you're in Thai Town unless you're looking for it, since it's only about six blocks long.

"The Valley"

There are many valleys including Conejo and San Gabriel, but only one "THE Valley". When we use this term, we are referring to the San Fernando Valley, home of cheaper rent, strip malls, hot temps, and porn. Did you see "Boogie Nights?" That's San Fernando Valley, right there, baby!

Are you South of the Boulevard or north? "The Boulevard" in that context refers to Ventura Boulevard which stretches across the whole region. It matters. The south offers large houses along curvy roads along the hill; North is probably where you'll live and spend most of your time.

However you get over the hill, anywhere you first land is included in this term – Reseda, Van Nuys, Sherman Oaks, or Studio City. Go further west into Encino, Woodland Hills, Thousand Oaks, and beyond, and it's a different world than "The Valley". That's the West Valley and is as hot as the devil's armpits, but you'll probably have a pool, and a family. You'd *better* have a pool. (Families are optional.)

Each area has subtle differences in its personality. But there's so much up there including both Peruvian chicken places AND Palestinian chicken places that you'll never need to venture back over the hill should you be so inclined.

Toluca Lake

This is a small area along the portion of Riverside Drive which is right next to Burbank. Bob Hope lived here and the zip code is pricier than its neighbors, but quiet and comfy with convenient access to the 134 and 101 freeways.

There *is* an actual lake, but it lies within a walled-in community that houses celebrities. For the common folk, you get a Chipotle two and a half miles away from another Chipotle.

Venice

Do you have tattoos? Hate wingtips but love flip flops or don't own any toed footwear whatsoever? Like to smoke weed? Enjoy skateboarding and/or surfing? Prefer your hair bleached? Then welcome home!

After Santa Monica gets seedier, you cross into Venice. And even though it's only a matter of the thin line separating the two, the vibe shifts considerably. You'd be surprised. There's a more hippy feel in Venice. And everyone has glaucoma . . . or something that requires medicinal marijuana . . . or *any* marijuana. Dreadlocks, tie-dye, bare feet are more prevalent. The drum circle on Sundays is a typical example of this type of free culture.

Westchester

Next to LAX, it contains homes with nice-sized yards and there are dogs everywhere, but there's no development so it feels like a city stuck in the 50s. The opening scene of *Six Feet Under* was filmed there, so . . . there's that.

West Hollywood

This is the center of the LGBT universe and provides the spectacle that is the Halloween parade which attracts tens of thousands of revelers. Another large demographic in WeHo is Russians, who generally reside east of Fairfax.

It's hip and becoming hipper with a gentrification movement raising rents and healthy dog-friendly restaurants popping up all over town.

WeHo is also a leader in handing out parking violations. (Seriously, you will get a ticket if your tires are not turned correctly.) It's crammed into the area between Beverly Hills and Hollywood and bumper-to-bumper traffic during peak travel times, and still several miles from the freeway (the 101).

In case you were wondering, this is where you'll find the Sunset Strip.

West Los Angeles

If you like living near the beach but don't want to pay beach prices, then West LA is for you. It borders Santa Monica, Brentwood, Westwood, and Century City, but doesn't have the same pretense. In fact, it's kind of a catch all of nationalities from the Little Tokyo area I mentioned earlier to a small section of shops with signs in Spanish. It's closer to the rest of Los Angeles while still being on the west side, so it possesses the best of all worlds to many people.

Westwood

It's just on the eastern side of the 405 freeway which, to many, represents "too far east". This is where you'll find the University of California – Los Angeles (UCLA) and also an area called "Little Persia" or "Tehrangeles" which is on Westwood Boulevard between Wilshire and Pico.

And More. . .

I've left out a bunch of neighborhoods and districts throughout Los Angeles County, such as Cheviot Hills, Valley Village, Lincoln Heights, West Adams, and much of the parts east to northeast of Los Angeles, but it's a huge area to cover and I figure you've got enough options to start your apartment search.

When you are looking, just be wary that not all apartments have kitchens. The rule of thumb is that a "bachelor" apartment has no kitchen, a "studio" has no bedroom, and a "one-bedroom" has all three, but may not have a roof. (Just kidding. All apartments come with a roof.) That said, not all rental advertisements are labeled accurately (honestly). If you intend to rent a place before you move out here, have a current resident check out the place for you, if possible.

PRONUNCIATION

Los Angeles is an American city with Mexican ancestry. Hence, some proper nouns are of the Spanish tongue, and some are spoken with an Anglo accent. Others are even more messed up. Learn the proper pronunciation so you won't seem like an outsider.

- Cahuenga - cah-WHEN-ga
- Calabassas - cal-a-BASS-ass
- Cannes - CAN (technically, this is in France, but so many people talk about it in Los Angeles that you'll want to be ready with the proper pronunciation)
- La Brea - La BRAY-ah
- La Jolla - La HOY-ah
- Los Feliz - Los FEE-liz (though half the population says "Los feh-LEEZ" which is the proper Spanish pronunciation for "the happy". You can also choose to call it "Lois, Feel These" as my friend Dave does, but then, Dave is not very well-regarded by society.)
- Pasadena - Pass-a-DEE-na
- Pico - PEE-co
- Rodeo - Ro-DAY-oh (or RO-dee-oh, depending on where you are. The first pronunciation refers to the famous one in Beverly Hills, the other to the one no one ever thinks about.)
- San Diego - San Dee-AY-go
- San Pedro - San PEE-dro (not as you would say the name Pedro, oddly)
- Sepulveda - Seh-PULL-veh-da
- Tejunga - Teh-HUNG-ah
- Tijuana - Tee-ah-WAN-ah
- Wilshire - WILL-sher

The good news is, many people get confused and you may not be corrected.

GET TO KNOW IT

When you arrive, just spend a day or two driving around town to get to know the place. It'll all seem the same at first, one big street after another but, eventually, you'll get a feel for it. You'll eventually know if it's La Cienega or La Brea that's east of Fairfax, which San Vicente is the one you want, how far Moorpark goes until it runs into

Riverside, what the heck does National think it's doing, and all the other quirks.

CONCLUSION

Set up meetings, plan to attend social gatherings, and begin developing your network of friends and allies, even before you set foot on the boulevards.

Many people come to Hollywood with the intention of making it big and then moving away. A friend of mine advised me to live in Hollywood as if this is where I wanted to be, where I planned to be, and where I loved to be through the foreseeable future. This . . . is. . . home.

If you have one foot back home, with three or four trips a year planned, you're less likely to succeed here. Make this move with your eyes forward and hit the ground running!

CHAPTER 3 - THE PLAYERS

INTRO

Now that you're here, we might as well learn about the people you'll be surrounded by. Who are these beams of light and energy that power the industry?

The first rule (and this is the first rule I ever learned from an industry big-shot): No one knows ANYTHING. This includes me. I may be right, but you may have the exact opposite experience which flies in the face of convention and thus renders my advice and opinion invalid.

KNOW THIS: No one knows anything. And neither do you.

This phenomenon happens frequently just to keep you off balance. It's what keeps you in LA; the fact that anything could happen at any time and anyone who is wrong may actually be right.

The moral of that phrase is, when anyone gives you the definitive end-all, be-all conclusion, they are talking out of their butts. Everyone comes at you from a different place but this won't stop them from preaching the Gospel anyway. Speaking of which, let's get to know these people as you'll be seeing a lot of them in the coming days, months, years, and decades.

WRITERS

No better place to start, right? Every scripted project starts with a writer. The writer is the most important person in any production because without anything written, there is no production. Still, a writer is also the first to get screwed, whether it's by changing their scripts, stealing their scripts, or forcing them to sit in the back of a shoot quietly with no input whatsoever as their words are bastardized.

Everyone is a critic of your work and, every step of the way, you have to fight to have your vision remain intact against a barrage of network and studio notes that range from the idiotic to the helpful via the completely absurd.

But writers can also be paid very well. You can make a great living AND you will never be hounded by any fans, unless those fans are other writers to whom you are a superhero.

If you are a "coffee shop writer" (and you will find every coffee shop has dozens), find your favorite hang outs and become a regular. Some important criteria include whether or not the spot has Wi-Fi, tables, comfy chairs, accessible free parking, and the most important thing: outlets. If you're gonna be there a while, you'll need to plug in.

The real scourge of the writer, however, is non-writers. Many of them won't understand your life and will think you're a slug. To others, it looks like you're just putzing around struggling for ideas. Inevitably, every writer has had this conversation – *"Hey, I have a great idea for a story. Do you want to write it with me?"*

Those words are like nails on a chalkboard to a writer. Then they compound it with, *"I'm bringing it to you because I'm an idea man, not a writer,"* as if there is some value in their skill.
Where to begin? So you've asked to write it "with" me, but admitted to not being a writer. So you're basically asking me to write it alone.

Laypersons (I like referring to non-writers as laypersons because it makes the writing profession seem like some sort of divine or noble profession) think when we're done with a project, a writer says, "I'm done!" and then sends it somewhere in exchange for immediate money. Simple.

Being an "idea man" is grating as well, since it implies that a writer does not have any ideas of his/her own. If anyone says, *"I'm a writer, but just have no ideas to write"*, well, then you're not a writer.

"I'm a surgeon, but have never operated on anyone." Yep, you are *not* a surgeon.

Here's the thing: Writers have to feel passionate about a project, otherwise it's a chore (which it typically is even if we are passionate about it). They have to wrap their heads around it. Now, if they get paid, it's a different beast.

New writers will start by working on "spec" (which is short for "speculation"). The only difference is, they are passionate about these ideas. They are very reticent to work on something that doesn't depict their soul . . . again, unless there's money involved. And even then, some writers still want to avoid this and focus on their *art*.

There's a difference of opinion about when you can declare yourself a writer. You will run into people who say you are *not* a writer unless you've earned money for your work. These people are entitled to their opinions. My opinion is that they should all be thrown into a flaming pit with all reality TV execs.

If you are writing (and I'm not talking tweets or funny e-mails), but are diligently working on projects for no money with no guarantee of production or publication, then you ARE a writer, one who writes. That said, writing is a progressive verb, so you must write continuously. It's not like the President of the United States who can stop doing it and still be called "Mr. President".

You can find courses on every aspect of writing – crafting the perfect first ten pages, how to write funny, 3-dimensional characters, selling your script – and consultants, writing groups, and script coverage folks to help you all over the place. The key is to start writing and never stop. With practice and a little luck, you will succeed.

The Writer's Guild Foundation library is a wonderful resource for scripts to read and books on scriptwriting: www.wgafoundation.org. Half of writing is reading, the other half is writing . . . and the third half is watching. Read scripts and watch finished products in order to write them.

The Writer's Guild's website is www.wga.org.

ACTORS

The typical joke is, "Oh, you're an actor! Which restaurant do you work at?" Actors, just so you know, are NOT "real people". When casting calls go out that say they want "real people", this means NOT actors.

The subset of actors in Los Angeles may be the most populous of all the industry players. Even people who *aren't* actors may be actors. Acting, as a process, can actually be done in your spare time, as a back up to something else. (Scientifically speaking, it's not rocket science.) But frequently, you get out of it what you put into it.

My general physician was in a commercial once. Imagine my surprise when I heard his voice on the television in my living room. He wasn't bad. He played himself. And considering how he regularly misdiagnosed my ailments (the hernia I never had and the huge tumor on my chest X-ray that was just a blot on the film), one might say he was a better actor than a doctor. Wait . . . was he even a doctor who acted or an actor *playing* a doctor?

As an actor, you're always performing, showing people who you are, because you never know who is going to provide you with that break or opportunity.

Your job is to stay in practice: practice your auditioning, practice breaking down scenes, practice rehearsing, appear in as many productions as you can. This is without getting paid. When you get good at doing it for free, eventually, you'll get paid for it. The same goes for anything, really, but for actors, there's so much thankless, criticized work that you have to enjoy the process first before you get rewarded. And even then, rewards may be few and far between.

It's not as glorious as you may have read. You submit for roles, drive all over town for auditions where casting directors apologize for running behind after you stressed out trying to be on time, tell them, "Hey, no problem," then leave it up to the people for whom you just danced to decide whether you succeeded or not by not actually telling you whether you succeeded or not.

You are out to impress everyone, from agents that can rep you and get you in front of casting directors who will pass you along to producers and maybe executives.

But you can control some of this. Actors can be, shall we say, unique personalities. And that can be welcomed in the casting room, but casting directors will tell you not to be too weird. Don't make them feel like their lives are in danger if the role calls for some violence. (It happens more often than you would think.) Be happy to be there. Just be professional. And for heaven's sake, don't shake their hands.

They are rooting for you. So just go on your audition and then forget about it the second you are out the door. The curse of the masses is that you always give your best audition in the car on the ride home.

You can't control their final decisions which can drive you mad; all you can do is focus on what you can control. All you can do is be the most qualified "you". Promote yourself, maintain your look, update your headshots, attend showcases, practice auditioning, get to know writers who could write something for you, write something for yourself, and never let them see you have a bad day.

The randomness of it all can tax you mentally. People study acting for years. And then they get a commercial agent based on their look and whether or not the agent already represents someone who looks like them. Training is a bonus. No training, and a unique look is even better. If you don't freeze up on camera, you're golden!

And then you look at the breakdowns (the breakdowns are your friend) that describe what they're looking for. Thousands of head shots come in. If you have a comedy background and a well-defined look (hippy, dad, bodybuilder, etc.) you'll get some bites. But if you have a skill (circus performer, long-distance runner, cellist), you are in high demand! All that training your friend who doesn't play an instrument did? Ha! No sense in that.

Sometimes the best acting skill you can have is knowing where to look during an audition and not freezing up on camera.

Acting is probably the most expensive endeavor of all – you need a ready supply for actor showcases, workshops, classes, new headshots, actor website subscriptions, and then anything you need to keep up your look. This includes hairstyling to a selection of clothes. What image are you going for? And if you decide to change your look, that's more headshots and/or clothing. And then when you finally get to join the Union, that's more money. It's pricey, but the benefits and pay scale makes it worth it.

There are many avenues an actor might take – commercials, sitcom, drama, theatre – and each has a different skill set, and different instruction. Stay focused. Choose one or two avenues and give it all you've got. Don't spread yourself too thin.

The goal for all working actors is to get into the SAG-AFTRA union. (The two bodies merged and formed one superpower at www.sagaftra.org.

If you are not SAG-eligible, you can sign up for extra work and get vouchers from work you've done. Sign up at Central Casting: www.centralcasting.com.

Voice Actors

There is a subset of actors who you don't see, but only hear. They are voice actors. This is an entirely different beast. Even the most successful may go unrecognized by the masses . . . until they speak.

The problem they face now is that on-screen actors are moving in on their territory, having realized that it still pays well but with better hours. It was an easy decision for them. They don't need to spend hours in a make-up chair, and they can show up in their pajamas if they want, and will be done at a reasonable hour.

Voice acting requires a slightly different skill set, such as the need to convey every emotion and every thought through one's vocal chords. It's a different discipline with an entirely specialized roster of players; there are different agents, coaches, teachers, workshops, showcases, casting directors, and executives for voice acting specifically.

If you get into it, you'll have several different subsets you can pursue – narration, commercial, animation, industrial, e-learning, video games, apps, mobile games, promo, and trailers. Each one requires a nuanced read.

The good news is that you can save on headshots but, in order to get started, you will need a "demo reel", one that is expertly produced and has you doing various reads. These can be actual productions you've done or, more than likely, will include spots you created to make people *think* you've done all these productions. It's one of those unwritten games between agents and actors. They know you haven't done the work, but they just want to hear your voice and abilities. (As if you weren't already spending enough on acting.)

If you choose to pursue both on-screen acting and voice acting, remember that you are spreading yourself thinner since the classes you need to take and the people you need to impress are not the same.

AGENTS/MANAGERS

Contrary to popular belief, being an agent is actually the oldest living profession – *not* prostitution. Fun fact: an agent was in the Garden of Eden with Adam and Eve. *"Oh, yeah, the apple's fine. Take it. I see big things for you once you grab that apple."*

My friend and I used to sing a song about agents to the tune of *Cheek to Cheek.*

> *Agents, I love agents,*
> *They're sincere, they're sweet, they mean just what they say*
> *I think I'll take a lunch with one . . . today.*

That's all we got, but I'm sure there's a Broadway musical in there somewhere. (Off Broadway?) Anyway, it made us laugh because we always hated talking to them. You never know what the truth is.

To be fair, they are just as panicked as you are, only with less creative talent. If they guess wrong, they don't get paid either, so they are wary about signing their client up for projects, or taking on new clients. If they don't find someone good, they're doomed. And if you don't earn them something soon, you may be on the out. They have to move on. But it takes time, and a good agent is a patient agent.

Agents are there to make the deal for you and charge you ten percent for their services. If it wasn't for their contacts, you could hire a lawyer to make the deal for you and save five percent. Managers, on the other hand, spend more time cultivating your talent and giving you direction as they seek out jobs for you. Either way, you're paying for their connections. And you spend countless hours trying to secure one.

Your family will ask, *"Can't you just hire an agent?"* The way it works is backwards. As an artist, you hire the agent, but the agent decides if they will work for you. So basically, they are hiring you.

You spend all your time getting someone to notice you and then when you finally get them, you are so happy that you don't realize that they suck, or that they're not right for you. Just because they are in this position doesn't mean they're good. (Even a broken clock is right twice a day.) You have to find one that you respect and one that respects you in return.

If you succeed, this will be the first person you thank. As you struggle, or they do not return your calls, they will remain pond scum.

If you happen to become an agent or manager, you can expect long hours, hot tempers, stressful days, calls at nights, work on the weekends, power lunches, myriad meetings, phone calls, professional business attire and, naturally, a super high turnover rate. Expect to start in the mail room or at a lesser agent's desk as an assistant, and you can move up very quickly if you don't screw up (see: turnover rate). And that's if you still want to be there after a few weeks of all the elements I mentioned.

There are big agencies and small agencies. As talent, usually you'll start smaller and outgrow them as you make a name for yourself. You'll be grateful for more personal attention at a smaller agency early on.

You can go online to find agents and managers. Always verify that they're accurate as the profession is a very fluid one with lots of turnover.

EXECS (Suits)

Let the battle for supremacy begin! Agents and executives locked in a power struggle, trying to understand the other, and deciding whether or not to believe anything the other says.

These suits work at a network or a studio level or in a production company with access to the networks or studios. But we're concerned with the first two, primarily for their veto power. They are the gatekeepers, and are as paranoid as anyone. One wrong call on a project and they can be fired. They may also need to be wary of other execs. It's recommended they schedule regular checkups with their doctors in order to check for stab wounds in their backs.

Many executives are people that have risen through the ranks and they may understand how the industry works. But understanding how the industry works and knowing what is high quality work are two different things, and this contributes to the friction between execs and creatives as both possess their own ideas on projects.

Like everyone else, execs are shooting darts at a board. This explains why you'll watch a TV show and ask, "*Who allows this stuff to be on television?!*" Remember, there are literally thousands of show ideas being pitched and only a few are chosen, which makes it all the more baffling when you see something that sucks.

Execs represent the final word on a script. They give notes which infuriate the writer and then the writer either addresses all these notes, or makes the exec think the notes have been addressed with a little two-step.

STAND-UPS/IMPROVISERS

Stage shows you're most likely to see or participate in fall under the categories of either stand-up or improv. Whereas stand-up is referred to as "work" ("*Are you working tonight?*"), improv is called "playing" ("*Do you want to play tonight?*"). It's fun and you are part of a team. You live and die together. Stand-up, on the other hand, is lonely. You kill or bomb alone (such violent terms, too).

In this day and age, everyone and their mother does improv at some point in time. It used to be only improvisers would take improv, but now it's a skill for actors, writers, and non-industry professionals just looking to be more spontaneous and come out of their shells. Second City, Upright Citizens Brigade, Improv Olympic and, the most famous of all, The Groundlings, all have consistently filled classes and popular shows.

And Improv *is* a skill. Yes, you are saying words off the top of your head, but there are tricks to be able to do that well. It takes practice to reach great levels, but once there, you will find work consistently.

On a grammatical note, if you ever write someone and tell them you are in a class, just know that you are "improvising" and not "improving." (Though you may, in fact, be improving at improvising.)

Improvisers are typically fun, friendly people accustomed to working unselfishly as part of a team. Stand-ups, on the other hand, are a different breed. The die-hard stand-ups are cynical, troubled personalities deep down. Successful ones are able to keep this side buried. If they continue to flounder, this persona is heightened. In fact, sometimes, even the successful ones cannot outrun their demons.

In Los Angeles, stand-up shows are not what you'd imagine. There are shows every night at the major comedy clubs, but these shows are not the classic Opener/Middle Act/Headliner that you'd see at "clubs and colleges across the country". These are showcase rooms where talent, and I use that term loosely as we'll discuss in a moment, perform their best material.

If you'd like to reach that point, you can start by showing up at an "open mic" to get your sea legs underneath you as you try out material. Open mics can be found anywhere: coffee shops, restaurant patios, laundromats, karaoke bars, etc. Usually the audience is made up solely of other comics who are not the biggest laughers in the world (because they are either focused on their own material or on how to turn your material *into* their material).

Then, you'll graduate to "bringer rooms" where the crowd is filled with guests you and the other performers on the bill invite. These are most shows.

Of a show with thirteen "stand-ups" on the bill, you may come across a range of people who are alternately really into stand-up, too poor to afford a therapist and so are griping on stage, or were recommended to try stand-up by a friend because they are "funny." Many of these are actors whose agent recommended they try it once and simply recite a monologue. That said, you may also find the next Jim Carrey among all the mediocrity.

All shows feature comic after comic in a seemingly endless parade. The audience has to frequently readjust their focus as each new act takes the stage which takes its toll after about ninety minutes. You'll remember that you enjoyed one comic or two and maybe recall a few jokes that tickled you, but won't be able to remember the comic's name.

The point being, if you have your sights set on stand-up, there's a lot of crap you have to rise above. If you're brilliant, it will be quick and less painful. If you're solid, but not flashy, then hang in there. It could take a while. Mold your personality to a stand-up's lifestyle, which is more nocturnal. Meet and befriend as many of the more serious performers as you can who will always inform you of the best places to "get up".

It's been said, and I believe this is true for the most part, that LA is not a place to start being a stand-up. It's where you come to *stop* being a stand-up. This means you have already honed your act somewhere, whether that be on the road or in your hometown club, and you're looking to make television bucks instead of dealing with audiences and club bookers and the grind of the business.

Stand-ups have to come up with material constantly. The performing is necessary to develop a mix of words and attitude.

If improv is your bag, frequent the theaters and perform as much as you can. In fact, you can also get "workout groups" together at someone's house on the side. The development of this craft comes from hours and hours of just doing it.

PRODUCERS

You too can be a producer with just a phone and a business card! (And the business card is optional.)

You may ask yourself, "What does a producer do?" This question has stumped the great philosophers of ancient Greece up to the very people who claim to be producers.

Essentially, the producer is the one who brings the elements of a project together – locations, permits, funding, the script, a crew, a cast, and everything else needed to bring it to you. "The organizer" is a fair synonym to describe a producer. And there are different roles that can make someone a producer. There may be different producers for each task in order to divvy up responsibilities.

A producer can be creative, the one who wrote the script or gives the notes; or good with budgets; or simply someone with a wad of dough who wants to break into Hollywood. There's a lot of money out there, and it's thrown around at garbage a lot, but it's still difficult to secure capital for such a speculative proposal as a movie or TV show.

Child birth is a miracle, but getting any type of creative project made dwarfs that every time. Employing the necessary crew, doing it on a schedule that works for the cast, and keeping it within a budget takes a perfect storm of fortune. Then you'd like it to be good, but hey, let's not get greedy.

Of course, what would the profession be without its own guild? www.producersguild.org.

For those looking to approach a "prod co" (production company), as they're called, there's a whole book filled with them. Get yourself a Hollywood Creative Directory. (An updated version is released about twice yearly as information is constantly changing, so just keep that in mind.)

DIRECTORS

Directors can come from anywhere – film school students, actors ready to start giving direction instead of taking it, someone with a camera and some free time. Everyone wants to direct.

There's an art to it that many people don't understand. The director collaborates with his or her director of photography to see what they can do with a frame and with the actors to see what kind of performance they can get. They are the conductors of any production.

In film, the director is the maestro. It's his or her vision which is why, "A Clint Eastwood Film" is the first thing that appears on screen.

In television, a director makes sure everyone is on the same page, but the vision is that of the showrunner. This explains why all shows have the same look and feel from week to week, even as they rotate through different directors.

If you want to become one, it would behoove you to get some training, such as in the Assistant Directors Training Program, and working your way in and up that way. Sure, you can just take your camera out for a spin and put something together, but the more you know, the better your product will be able to stand out from the crowd.

Hey, here's something you may not have known – directors have their own guild too! www.dga.org.

SINGERS

Like everything, becoming a singer is a battle. Open mics, permits to perform on the street, and recording studios make Los Angeles a great city in which to showcase. Whether or not you are discovered depends on all the usual factors of luck, connections, and talent.

Like stand-up, it is not necessarily a place to start your career. You can be a great singer from anywhere. (Especially with the slew of *American Idol*-type shows out there.) But it comes down to proximity. You never know who is going to see you.

Lisa Loeb became famous because she was Ethan Hawke's neighbor when he was making *Reality Bites.* He put her song in the movie and she achieved greater success after that.

There may be dozens of Lisa Loebs out there that we'll never hear. Just go down to Third Street Promenade and you'll see wonderful musicians. There is a benefit to being in town as opposed to across the country that allows you to experience this fortuitous break, but you still have to rise above the muck (which you'll also find on Third Street Promenade).

Give out samples to whoever asks for them. Your music may be a Top 40 hit, or it may be used as background music, or in video games, or as a theme song, or in a screenplay. You never know who's looking for what you have to offer.

ALL THE REST

Hollywood is a place for all sorts of production people and ancillary help. Do you dream of working on a production? You can become a teamster, though that's as difficult a union as there is to break into. Do you want to do hair and make-up (HMU) for a living? Set design? Work alone in a darkened room glaring at a monitor as an editor? Maybe you don't know specifically and just have a desire to be involved somehow. Watch the end credits of a movie or TV show. All those jobs, all those titles are available to you.

It's also competitive, but perhaps not as much as the careers I mentioned earlier in the chapter. Whatever you choose, do it for free (or "on the cheap") at first, learn the ins and outs, get a mentor, ask questions and, eventually, you'll be called up to the majors. Meet producers and offer your services to film schools who need low cost help. And always, no matter how rinky-dink the production, *always be professional.*

CONTINUING EDUCATION PROFESSIONALS

Hollywood is the type of town where it'd be nice if you arrived with a formal education from a place of higher learning, but it's not necessary. You may have gone to school for four years and studied television and film, but did you learn about how the industry works from industry professionals in an industry setting? There are always seminars and courses being offered on every little piece of minutiae that will give you the "definitive" answers from the people who have succeeded in some way shape or form.

When people who have been working are no longer working, or are on hiatus from working, or are supplementing their working, they will be happy to offer their services for a price.

Teachers

Aside from all the one-time webinars and four to six week courses explaining any and every aspect of the industry, you have the local colleges which offer extension courses. UCLA extension is one of the most popular, but look around, you'll find opportunities everywhere.

New knowledge is always useful. Costs do add up though and you may reach a saturation point on a particular subject, in which case, you'll just have to find another subject. You'll never be at a loss.

If you did not study the industry before moving out to LA and have no formal training, you'll still be able to piece together a very thorough education in a relatively short period of time. In fact, though I loved my college experience, I thought that the money could also have been well spent living here and learning about the way Hollywood works. (That's what this book is for, I guess.)

Consultants

Already know what you're doing but need a little one-on-one time? You can always find a consultant to work with you. Even if they don't officially call themselves consultants, I'm sure you can find people with a modicum of experience that would be happy to take your money in order to give you an hour of their time or for a series of consultations. Acting coaches, script consultants, voice gurus, life advisors, (comedy punch up guys such as the author of this book – wink, wink), and so on are here for you. Depending on their level of experience, the prices can be steep for an hour.

There are people who give you great advice and guide you when you need it, but remember, there's no guarantee that this knowledge will help you get ahead. It may simply provide peace of mind. Always get recommendations from people you trust that have used the consultant's services.

BULLSHIT ARTISTS

In a town like Hollywood, where money is desired above all else, there are many who prey on the naïveté and innocence of others in order to make more money. These other artists in this town are of the "bullshit" variety.

A friend was just telling me about this guy that sat next to him at a coffee shop recently. He used a delicate European accent when responding to a pretty woman then, after she left, he got on his cell phone and started talking like one of the Beastie Boys.

Remember, this is a town of performers. Be wary.

Vultures

There is someone out there who can help you (and everyone in this town needs *some* help), but he also knows he can help himself more. A vulture is anyone who circles those in need and will gladly take their money. It doesn't matter if it's a seedy guy using his one bedroom apartment as a casting office or agents in reputable agencies, you're always going to be a target given your need for guidance and assistance.

For example, your agent, the one you've spent a lot of time wooing, finally decides to "take a chance on you". But before they do, they want you to take courses, get new headshots, and spend more money. And what, are you going to say no? You say yes. They send you to a friend of theirs (the "only one" who can take headshots properly) and receive a monetary kickback for the referral. And the cycle continues. Whether or not you book anything or not, your agent has already made money off you and you're in the hole.

It's cynical to think, but there may be times when you feel you are finally connecting to someone in the industry that they may just be figuring out how to fleece you.

Now, you will have to spend money (success ain't free), but spend it wisely. The old adage of "You have to spend money to make money" should be referred to judiciously. That means taking care to properly vet the myriad of hucksters who tell you what you want to hear and the very

57

service they are offering. *Do I need this service? What can I realistically expect to get from this service?*

If you deal in intellectual property (scriptwriters and auteurs), always, always, always copyright it. This will protect you from the vultures. It isn't that expensive and the US Copyright Office has a page where you can do this online: www.copyright.gov.

And then there are those who are not necessarily vultures because they are not looking to take anything except your time, but you should also be wary of those who ask you to collaborate with them when they present the offer as *"When we're done, I'll share the profits with you."*

That's great, but it's so difficult to make a profit off a creative idea so unless you are sure the proposal will make money, you should consider how valuable your time is before jumping at that offer. No one ever says, *"Hey, if you design my website for me, I'll split all the ad revenue with you once I reach one million views"* or *"Can you put a musical on for the community? We'll split the door receipts."* You'd like some of the windfall up front, thank you.

Oh, and ask to get it in writing. Anyone who balks at that is trouble.

Big Talkers

KNOW THIS: I don't know anything, and neither do they.

(It's the same phrase from the beginning of the chapter, but presented differently.) If they swear they know, they're wrong. Oh, sure, they may be right at some things, but you can't say you will be with any type of certainty initially. Hollywood is about playing the percentages so people who talk with conviction are just reciting the odds. It's up to you if you want to buck the odds or play it safe.

Question anyone who swears they know FOR SURE and anyone who says it's a no-brainer. If anyone says, "just" when it comes to a time prediction, as usually pertains to production ("It'll just take four hours") doesn't understand production. Production is like moving in that way. *I've only got*

a box spring and two end tables. It'll just take an hour or so. CUT
TO: Midnight and you're only halfway through.

Image is everything so people will show big and talk big,
even if the majority of them can't back it up. They drive cars
they can't afford. *You can see how successful I am by my car . . .
(which I rented earlier today just to bring to our meeting).* Most people
who are truly successful don't need to talk big. It's those who
crow about their qualifications that you need to wonder
about.

TAX GUY (OR GAL)

Not to overlook one of the most important people in your stable,
every artist needs to have a tax guy that can take full advantage of the
rules for entertainment professionals. Artist taxes are different from
real people taxes and, to that extent, every tax guy is not equal.

When you're staring down the barrel of a large donation to your
greedy and unworthy government, just know that you can turn the
tables and get a check *from* (or at least send a lesser donation to) your
greedy and unworthy government. As an artist, you can deduct a lot
of things you may not have known.

Ask around and find someone who knows what you can do come
April 15. I've been surprised to learn that one can deduct your cell
phone bill as a business expense, Netflix bill as research, and haircuts
(for an acting career), as well as script consultations, seminars,
showcases, etc.

This doesn't even include lunches with friends where we'd talk
shop.

It was always funny to sit across the table from a fellow stand-up.
The meal would end and we'd split the cost, but one of us would
inevitably say, *"Did you see the new Sandler movie?"*

"Yes."

"Good, we talked about comedy," and he'd snatch the receipt and jot
down, *"business lunch with Andy".*

CONCLUSION

Hollywood is a city where everyone is reliant on others for
success. Each player has different motivations, a different mindset,
and an entirely different make up. Getting to know who you're
dealing with will help. The executives can be the final say in whether a
production gets off the ground or not, but even then, they are

hoping the cast and crew pull it off, otherwise, they may not have a job in the morning.

And because of that, there are people who hold control and people who are at the discretion of these people. And all of these people are on edge, hoping that they'll be allowed to thrive and create for their egos, their legacies, their paychecks, or just for their sanity.

It's really a collaboration, one where everyone is out for their own benefit, but realize that they can do better playing nicely with others. Join creative collaborations such as Film Independent www.filmindependent.org or We Make Movies www.wemakemovies.org, or check out Cinefamily www.cinefamily.org in order to immerse yourself into the film culture with other film lovers. That's how you network and ultimately build your *own Lonely Island* or *Good Neighbor Stuff*.

CHAPTER 4 - THE RIGHT MENTALITY

INTRO

Having the right mentality makes all the difference. Los Angeles has a daily influx of multi-talented people and, since appreciation of these people is subjective, it stands to reason that talent isn't always the leading predictor of success. It can be very frustrating when you try to think logically - *I have a better education than him* or *I'm more classically trained* or *I work harder than she does.* The truth is, you just never know.

There are some very solid rules to building your mental foundation that I've found can help get you through the slow points.

THE RANDOMNESS OF SUCCESS

Some of the most talented people in this town may find less success than an untalented hack. Take commercial acting, for example. You may have studied acting at Julliard, done summer stock at Tanglewood, and been mentored by Sir Laurence Olivier himself, but still lose out on the gig for hemorrhoid cream to the goofy guy with the big belly and bushy beard. (To be fair, he's a riot!)

Why do some people rise to the top while others remain mired in mediocrity? Once you let go of any notion that this makes sense and just enjoy your experience, you'll be free to achieve whatever the universe has in store for you. (Yes, it sounds cheesy, but it's a better way to look at it and saves on therapy bills.) In the meantime, you show up with all the necessary tools to give the universe no choice.

THREE QUALITIES YOU NEED

In Hollywood, you meet people with the same dreams and desires as you. What separates them from you? Outside of creative styles and ideas, the success train needs three things in order to pull into the station:

1. Talent
2. Drive
3. Professionalism

Lacking any of those three can cause the gap between Future Hollywood Success Story and Hollywood Wannabe.

Talent

Be as good as you can be. Keep practicing, learning, improving, and we can assume the talent portion will work itself out. I have partnered with people who have missed one or all of these attributes and it's not fun. You become the workhorse and your coattails get scuffed.

Let's assume you do already have some talent. You've excelled somewhere before this, right? But so have a good portion of everyone else. Remember that Hollywood is a subjective town and you are not *so* good that you can just show up and be revered. Even if you are, your chances at success are not guaranteed. Let's say you're in the top echelon of your profession. It will still take some work to find your place among the others in the top echelon. Luck plays a mighty big role in things, but that's out of your control, so don't pay it any mind for the harder you work, the luckier you get.

Drive

I worked on a spec script with another writer once. In the beginning, he was gung ho. We brainstormed together and when the time came to write, we agreed to each write alternating scenes. I did scene one and submitted it to him to go along with his scene two.

When it came time for scenes three and four, I did scene three and he either became too busy or disinterested to continue. He threw some excuses at me.

KNOW THIS: No one wants to hear your excuses.

In the end, I scrapped his scene two and completed the script on my own, leaving his name off, naturally.

Understand that some ideas, whether they be your marketing plan, your edit of a project or script may not have the oomph you once thought they did. Sometimes it's after sleeping on it that you realize there are flaws. It's not going as easily as you thought. But if you believe in your goal, project, viral campaign, whatever, then do not leave it partially finished because you've already come this far. And you can't fix it until it's completed. So have the drive to finish it.

Professionalism

I hired an animator for another project of mine. He was talented and had the drive, but missed deadline after deadline. To make matters worse, he had an excuse every time he missed a deadline.

Hollywood is a town where, regardless of your talent, there are dozens of people with talent that can do the job comparably. No, it might not have your *signature flair*, but who cares when it's a matter of getting it done versus *not* getting it done?

You'd be very surprised when you hear what constitutes professionalism in this town. Showing up (on time preferably) and being likable. Boom! That's it! You're a professional.

Friends that I've spoken to who have spent time as production assistants talk of getting commended by their bosses for doing things as simple as being prompt and smiling when asked to get bananas or move a chair from one spot to another.

Don't take this for granted because what seems obvious to you, can be rocket science to your competition. Creative people don't always excel at technical, mundane details. And people with four-year degrees may feel they are above a certain task.

There's a difference between "work that's hard" and "hard work". The work you need to do is not hard, but it *is* hard work.

Remember, if you're the best in college, you are only competing against four years' worth of people. Now, in Hollywood, the pool of competition covers a dozen classes from hundreds of colleges. If you are an actor, you are going against everyone in your demographic; if you're writing, you are going up against basically everyone who has a computer, from upstart high schoolers who are already shooting their own stuff on Go Pro cameras to 70 year-olds who have been at it for decades. If you are looking to edit or work on set design, get in line. You can stand out simply by not screwing up.

KNOW THIS: Luck still plays a part in your success, but you can give luck a booster shot by having talent, drive, and professionalism.

THE MOST IMPORTANT FOURTH QUALITY

Wait, but you just said there were only three qualities I needed. Yes, I did. And I don't care what anyone says, you *are* a very astute reader.

There is, indeed, one other quality that trumps the other three and can make up for it if you lack any of the first three and that is [drum roll please!]. . . PRESENTATION. As Hollywood is about the superficial, you can cover up any weaknesses and flaws you may have by presenting yourself as someone with no weaknesses and flaws. That's why lots of people dress the part, or drive a car they can't afford.

Not knowing what you're doing is not as bad as looking bad doing it. It's a town where you can find yourself overwhelmed or out of your league at times. You gotta act like everything's cool, even as your peers and bosses may be running around like they're on the deck of the sinking Titanic. It could save your job, or even get you promoted.

TIPS FOR A POSITIVE MINDSET

It's hard to remain positive, especially when most of the replies you get come in the form of a rejection, but no one is going to suffer your failures. Feeling bad and moping won't help.

People are always posting motivational sayings on Facebook. Reading these little platitudes do help. They represent the supporters cheering you on during every step of the 26.2 mile marathon you're doing. So put a smile on your face and don't let anything discourage you. How can you do this?

Here are a few constant reminders you should take with you:

Be Confident, But not Cocky

Have confidence, but don't think you're better than everybody else. Respect the game because, as we've just learned, it's not always about being better.

To that end, don't be too humble either. Sell yourself, but don't try to fool people into believing you're better than you are because they won't fall for it. (Too many people have already tried this and the industry people are hip to it.) It's a tricky tightrope, but let your work speak for itself.

When in doubt, avoid downplaying yourself. Don't say, Well, I'm only a set designer. If you don't believe in your cause, no one else will. The more people (and I'm not talking about your friends) who respect your work, the more you'll know how good you really are.

Take Criticism Well

Be prepared to take criticism and learn from that criticism. The more people you connect with, the more feedback you'll be able to get. Granted, it's not always good criticism, but you need to know how to use it.

Always, ALWAYS take out the best commentary and the worst from your batch. And that includes the "constructive" advice from the bitter guy who thinks you've made a mistake. (Put advice like that aside and use it in your own book someday detailing the bad advice you've received on your rise to the top.)

Follow Your Bliss

What makes you happy? Is it the process of auditioning for commercials? Performing improv? Sitting in a dark edit bay with hours of raw footage or alone in a coffee shop with a fully-charged laptop?

First and foremost, do what makes you happy. If you're happy doing it, then you won't notice the slow strides you're making on a day-to-day basis. If you don't enjoy auditioning for commercials, then you definitely won't enjoy the rejection that comes with it.

Everyone wants to be successful. It's the enjoyment of the things needed to become successful that will make you successful.

Stay Flexible

Along those lines, if you are not making strides, such as getting closer to booking a gig or winning a contest, then you may want to refocus your game plan or reassess your skills. Hollywood has lots of doors that can let you in. Try shifting your sights to one of the other doors. Embracing the education process can be a good thing, presuming it's financially feasible and represents a step forward.

There's a tipping point for writers who have written dozens upon dozens of screenplays or actors who have been in front of every casting director in town before they should realize their style is not the style that Hollywood wants or the style that plays to their strengths. Unfortunately, there's no equity built up for continued loyal service.

Remember, if success is your ultimate goal, you're in it for the wrong reasons. It's for the love of the game. If you're enjoying what you're doing – writing, filmmaking, recording, acting, etc. – and can support yourself some other way, then by all means, keep at it.

Don't Be Envious

Focus on your own trajectory, not someone else's. Your quest has nothing to do with the next person's. Your failure is not predicated on their success and vice versa.

KNOW THIS: Everyone follows a different path and it's rarely dictated by logic.

Steven Spielberg has had quite an accomplished career, but (not to diminish his work) there are so many up-and-coming filmmakers with a boatload of Spielbergian talent that will never be recognized. Whatever combination of factors he had going for him provided the perfect storm to achieve his success quickly and keep it going. The good news: once you have one notch in your belt, it is easier to achieve more.

So don't be envious. In fact, it's always cool (at least, you should think it's cool) when you're connected to someone who makes it. At the very least, like talent tends to find each other. This indicates that you can make it too.

UPS & DOWNS

We tend to spend time focusing on all the success stories. After all, they are constantly being trumpeted throughout town and in pop culture magazines. There's such a steady and constant stream of successful people that they blend together. And that's a natural thing for most stars only shine brightly for a short period of time. Only rarely do we think to ask, *Hey, whatever happened to . . . ?* when someone is no longer on top.

Hollywood is a rollercoaster ride. If John Belushi knew this, he might be alive today. He only went through one up and one down. When *Animal House* hit, and then was followed up by a starring role in *The Blues Brothers*, he was on top of the world. But he hit a lull.

He went from being one of the hottest stars to being cast in crappy projects. He had no idea how to reverse course. As the story goes, he was so depressed that he relapsed into drugs and finally died at the Chateau Marmont along the Sunset Strip in Hollywood.

What he didn't know was he would have returned to the top in short order as his friend Dan Aykroyd was finishing work on a vehicle they would both star in. It was a little comedy called *Ghostbusters*, which found a different brilliant genius in Bill Murray and turned out to be one of the highest-grossing comedies of all-time.

Other actors will try to extend the highs by changing it up a little – comedians like Bill Murray, Steve Martin, or Jim Carrey will attempt a drama. Dramatic actors like Lloyd Bridges and Leslie Nielsen found themselves in absurd comedies like *Airplane!* which prolonged their careers and showed another generation of viewers a different side of themselves. But think of the many who found no success in diverting from the formula which brought them fame.

Learn to navigate the ups and downs. You'll get good news that leads nowhere and bad news that doesn't ruin everything as you thought it might. It's your job to stick it out; your cross to bear, so to speak. The ups will fade, as will the downs, but if you focus on the ups and ignore the downs, it will make your survival that much easier.

FOR THE SAKE OF KARMA

People will ask you for favors or assistance all the time. If you agree, just do it because you want to and not simply for the *sake* of karma. Once Karma knows that you are only being nice in an effort to "gain points," you will be shunned by the cruel and fickle mistress.

Do a favor, be kind, be complimentary because you genuinely mean it.

(Yes, karma is an abstract idea, but go ahead and test my theory . . . if you dare.)

AVOID THE JADED

You will come across these people all the time. Even successful (or moderately successful people can fall into this trap because they didn't quite make it to the level they envisioned). They bring negative juju to the table and should be avoided like the plague.

I took a workshop with an acting manager once. She asked us to tell her a little about ourselves. I mentioned I was a comedian from Boston. She flinched. Apparently, this was a bad idea on my part because she explained she had been married to a comedian from Boston and, by the sound of things, had not quite reconciled that part of her life yet.

I did a good comedic scene, got a lot of laughs from the class, and stood waiting for her thoughts. She didn't say a thing about my acting but, after a long pause, said, "You . . . do something with your mouth."

"Uh, okay, can you elaborate?"

"No. It's just you do something."

I found this funny because the one successful client she represented was known for his quirky delivery in which he *squints*. But given that she'd already pretty much made it known what she was going to think of me for reasons beyond my control, I didn't put any stock into it. (My acting teacher confirmed that I don't do anything out of the ordinary.)

Sometimes you just have to let people have their moment and not put any credence in them. If you let them, they will eventually poison your thoughts with *their* failures. That means, their experiences will inform their visions of what will happen to you though your paths are not related.

PREPARE TO BE SCREWED

There's a popular and discouraging phrase you might hear and that is, "You'll get screwed on your first project."

Now, there are different levels of being screwed. You may only get $100,000 whereas a more well-established artist could get a half-million. That's the GOOD kinda screwed.

But early in your careers, you may reach a point where a crappy deal is placed on the table. The crappy deal is still going to be better than your current non-existent deal. So you take it because you want to move forward.

It's a stepping stone. That is to say, if this deal gets you something for your resume, a connection, or a completed project you can be proud of, then that's great.

Now, if you're expecting to break the bank on your first project, well then, you're better off waiting for the six-figure deal with the major studio that you feel you deserve out of the gate. There are people who get these, but if you ever went to Vegas, would you gamble on the 0.000001% chance of coming through?

Of course, if you have an agent working for you and/or are in one of the guilds, then you will have a better shot at avoiding this pitfall.

CONCLUSION

Attitude accounts for most of your success in Hollywood (as the game is at least 50% psychological), for while you are battling as hard you can, the infrastructure is set up to beat you down. If you let it, you have lost.

You need to have the right philosophy about your involvement in the industry. Get up every day, do your work, don't let anyone else steer you off course, and let the chips fall where they may.

CHAPTER 5 - YOUR SUPPORT SYSTEM

INTRO

You are taking a risk in beginning your new life far from home, leaving your friends and family behind in the process. It can be mentally taxing to work on what is essentially a do-it-yourself project without a blueprint. There will be times when you'll question yourself, lament your mistakes, and consider quitting. That's when you need cheerleaders.

Now that you have your head on straight and are settled in, ready to make some hay, you need to put a support system in place.

FAMILY AND FRIENDS BACK HOME

Some of you will come here leaving nothing behind, perhaps as an escape from your past, but for those of you leaving a large collection of friends and/or family, making it in Hollywood and achieving your ultimate dream in spite of all opposition could be very important to those dear to you back home . . . almost as important as convincing you to move back home and be close to them for the rest of their lives (if they are anything like my mother).

Consider this – you've got guts. You're following your dream. Not many people can say they did that. Many wanted to, but perhaps chose a safer, more secure path. Maybe they got married and had kids early; maybe they landed a good-paying job quickly and selected that lifestyle instead. Having a dream is noble but following it is divine. (Unless it's to star in your own reality show, then you should seek therapy.)

Win or lose, more people will respect you than demean you. And if someday, you realize a different dream and move on from acting or whatever brought you out here, no one can fault you for trying. One platitude you'll hear again and again is *"You regret the things you don't do more than the things you do"*.

Of those close to you, your supporters will fall into three different categories:

Unwavering Supporters

I like to think that you will receive more positive reinforcement than negative from people connected to you. You're working for an entire village looking to claim you as their own. Never mind that they can't help you much, these unwavering supporters will be rooting for you like no other. (*You're following your dream and I admire that.*) For while you are scratching and clawing in LA, they are bragging about you back home. (*My friend/son/friend's daughter [insert your name here] is making it in LA.*)

Regardless of your *actual* success, you are making it in their eyes. They see you as a star, even as you may not agree. Soak it up because not everyone will be so unconditionally supportive.

Cautious Supporters

There are some who are not as effusive with their praise. They represent the realist and are not wired to take the leap without a net. They may love you, but want to protect you.

I'll never forget what my grandmother said to me a few years into my stand-up touring days. *"I think it's great what you're doing, Andrew, and I'm pulling for you 100% . . . now when are you going to get a job?"*

The words and advice of the cautious supporter can come off as undermining when taken out of context. They'll say, *"There's no question that you are going to make it, but you should have a fallback plan . . . for when you don't"*. But these people don't mean you any harm.

Maybe they feel they're protecting you, or maybe it helps them feel safe based on their experiences or philosophies. To you, it can be frustrating. Focus on the positive parts of their messages. My grandma only wanted the best for me and that meant a guaranteed salary.

Clueless Supporters

Then there are those who mean well, but can drive you crazy. They don't understand how to navigate Hollywood, but figure it has to be just like your hometown, population 7000. *Why can't you just call Steven Spielberg and tell him you're Jewish?*

They mean well, they really do, but they just don't get it. *"Can't you just hire an agent?"* they'll ask. They only want to help.

Just nod and smile and tell them you'll look into it. It's much easier than explaining how someone secures an agent in town. (Or better yet, buy them a copy of this book and let me explain it for you!)

Anti-supporters

And then, in every group, there's always one sourpuss who's looking to cut you down for whatever reason. Maybe it's your bitter Uncle Ned, or your hairstylist who always wanted to move to LA, but didn't have the confidence. You'll recognize who they are from the fact they say nothing complimentary about your life.

"Acting, huh? I always thought you'd make a great dentist", or *"People in LA are crazy. You don't want to be one of them."* You can't force them to shut up, so it's best just to ignore them.

Whereas most of the people in your life are great (hopefully), you need to immerse yourself among people who know exactly what you're going through.

FRIENDS IN LA

The support system you're likely to lean on most is composed of your LA peers. These are your cheerleaders, your mentors, your battalion mates, those on the front lines with you. They can take the form of fellow artists or good friends outside the industry who are not working on their own careers 24/7.

Helping others is a two-way street. And this is a journey which takes a village. Friends can keep you up to date on opportunities, do you favors, act as another pair of informed eyes for solid feedback, connect you with their network, and so on.

Of course, the word "friends" may be a little misleading in this case. Your fellow artists are more like coworkers, people you call if you need help in getting the job done. "Friend" may be accurate, but sometimes a little generous in the cases of those who introduce you at parties with, *This is my really good friend Bob . . . I'm sorry, what's your last name again, Bob?*

You'll need dozens of people in your contacts, if only a few on your speed dial, including Facebook friends you've only met once, but would like to keep tabs on. You might meet them at mixers, in classes, a peer group, at parties, or while watching a sporting event, and you'll connect with them for one reason or another. There are career support groups and regular meet ups where you can manufacture your team. Most of the time, you'll never talk to them again, but once you find someone you respect, and it's mutual, you'll have a supporter.

In effect, these people should be on your "mooch list". This is a list of qualified people you trust that can help you do what you need to do. If you need a film crew, you can refer to that list to find someone to hold the boom mic, someone with a camera, someone with lighting equipment, etc. If you don't know anyone, it's a sure thing that someone you know knows someone.

You're all going for the same thing – to achieve a life of doing what you love. Cheer them on and they'll cheer you on in return. If you can help them generously while continuing to cultivate your own process, you will have them at your disposal as well.

You might not spend lots of quality time with them, but they are there and that represents a tremendous resource. Try to connect with those you truly respect and enjoy at least twice a year, even if it's just with a personalized email, so you don't lose them as they're constantly gaining new contacts and, no doubt, flying in many different directions.

CONCLUSION

Once you have a good internal support system, a mix of people who are rooting for you and people who know exactly what you're going through, it'll take some weight off your shoulders. You have help. It's no longer you against the world. Your friends can pull you up as you pull them up.

People who challenge you, but don't question you, support you, but don't coddle you are your greatest asset.

CHAPTER 6 - EARNING A LIVING

INTRO

Chances are you won't get off the boat and be famous. Call me crazy, but you'll need to earn a living. Before you get THAT job, that reason you came to LA in the first place, you may need a job (or jobs) that will provide boring things for you, like food or a place to live.

In your head, you know exactly how it'll go – you'll use your charm and work ethic to make it after only a year, just as easily as you've done everything else in your life. Perhaps you'll get a job as a production assistant followed by a writer's assistant then you'll do your first story for the producers and become a story editor and finally, showrunner of the most popular show on TV.

Or maybe you'll showcase for a casting director and blow them away. They'll cast you in a guest star role, and a big network muckity-muck will think you stole the show and make you the star of their new pilot. Then, in your SECOND year . . .

And this is the way it's going to be because you're the type of person who succeeds whenever you set your mind to something. But it probably won't go exactly as you imagine. As I mentioned in chapter four, you have to remain flexible.

LEAVE YOURSELF OPEN

Your neighbor knows a guy who needs a production assistant on a commercial shoot for a day. You need the money so you take it. You'll continue to look for your perfect job the next day, you tell yourself. But then you do your typical great job (not to brag, but it's a curse being as efficient as you are) and they hire you for their next shoot and the next and the next and the next.

Now you've risen up the ranks and are getting paid well, but that includes long hours which prevent you from networking or even applying to jobs that would get you back on your career path. The good news is, you're in with the producer and meeting other commercial producers.

That's your world. For you see, though you always thought you'd be in sitcoms, it's all categorized as "production," and that includes myriad subgroups, both long-form and short. Sure you can still take other work, but this current job is taking up all of your time and you're exhausted the rest of the time. Plus, you'd still like to keep a social life and the bills keep coming.

Why give up on this job? After all, you're actually good at it.

A short time later, you're now the producer of these commercials and are hiring other kids who have just moved to town looking to work in sitcoms.

FUNDING FIRST

Yes, you can always be bold and leave your current job or look for a better one if it's that important to you but, early on, don't get caught up in your plan. You aren't in a position to be too picky. Finding a job is good since you need to live, but not all jobs are equal in providing you the time to do what you came here for.

You need funding for classes, for socializing (i.e. expanding your network), for submissions, promotions, and then the basics, just for life. To participate in the industry, you have more expenses than just happy hour and weekend trips that many nine-to-fivers have. Spend the first phase building your brand and enhancing your qualifications.

I had a full-time, office job and used to hate being interrupted at my office by guys wanting to talk about the previous night's game (this usually happened four or five times a day). It interrupted my "free time" when I was working on some project of my own that was (don't tell anyone) not job-related. They were merely interrupting their *real work* time.

But it paid well. So I needed to fake the job that ran counter to my goals while I stockpiled cash for five years. I invested extra into my 401k all the while carrying on conversation after mindless conversation about last night's game.

A JOB FOR YOUR FUTURE

Ideally, you can get a job that allows for your artist's lifestyle, leaving you with the freedom to audition, money for classes, or time to sing, write, paint, etc. It may not be a job that uses your college degree, but it could lead to something later, maybe with an added networking aspect, or insider status.

Get a job "in the industry" and then work your way up through the ranks: mail room, assistant, manager, director, vice president – and that might be a good way to meet people and show them you are professional. "Entry-level" is the term. Can you afford to start with an internship? It's highly competitive, but many people are eliminated from contention because they need to be paid. It doesn't always take "knowing someone" so you'll be able to find something.

The people you are bringing coffee or mail are the same people who oversee the hiring of a film cast and crew or the making of a television show. Before they need to know that you can perform whatever it is you came here to perform, they need to know you can show up, smile, follow directions, flavor their coffee properly, buy the "correct bananas" (yes, I was once questioned for buying the "wrong bananas"), and any other task a monkey could probably do as well.

Figure out what you need in order to succeed in your career. Do you need to get away for auditions? Do you need money to fund courses? An office with free photocopying and a postage machine for those cover letters? Do you need evenings free to have access to the recording studio? Are you a morning writer so a job that begins at 10 a.m. is the best?

For actors, the reason they gravitate toward jobs in the service industry such as in restaurants or catering is because it provides good money in a short period of time (at the better establishments) and allows flexible hours in order to get away for auditions.

It may seem like a 9-to-5 is counterproductive, but there are office jobs that allow you to take "long lunches" for auditions as many of your bosses are sympathetic to your course and even may have been in your shoes before. Ask them what their course has been and what they came to town to do originally.

Mainly, any job with off hours and flexibility could do. Something that when the clock hits quitting time, you don't have to think about, and while you're there, you don't have to exert too much brain power.

These jobs are good for any up-and-coming artist:

- Barista
- Server/host
- Catering
- Freelance anything
- Security

- Temp (though as someone new to every job, it's difficult to take time off before you've developed a rapport and people begin to know your name and like you)
- Substitute teacher
- Anything in the service industry (like dog walker, landscaping, house cleaning, construction, etc.)
- Bartender
- Retail (however, while the hours are flexible, you are pretty much afforded no freedom outside of your lunch break)
- Studio tour guide or Network Page
- Production assistant gigs could be good if they are not consistent. You work for a few days, make some good money (due to the long hours) and then have some time off, though much of that time will be spent trying to secure your next job. But you might realize you never want to do that job again.

I mentioned Central Casting before. Even if you are not an actor, this could be a good, easy way to pay some bills. The pay isn't great, but gives you some production experience – you can see how a set operates, the grind involved, and perhaps do some networking during your down time, which will be most of the time.

And those assistant jobs where your boss lets you get away are a dream come true for they may pay well *and* provide a great opportunity to network. I found my way into that situation first as a network page. (Several networks and studios have them.) It led to a position as an assistant to the executives.

THE "90/10" RULE

The industry is known for its "hurry up and wait" policy. This leads to the fact that 90% of the work is done in 10% of the time. So there's a lot of down time. Three hour lunches for your bosses (not for you) are not frowned upon. It's the other 10% of the time where all hell breaks loose and you think the entire infrastructure of Hollywood is going to crumble. It hasn't yet and probably will not in the near future. (At least, not from anything you do.)

So it bodes well that you can still have a solid full-time job (*with* benefits, whaaaaaaat?) while still pursuing your dream.

TAKING A JOB V. FOLLOWING YOUR BLISS

You may come to a point where you're offered a good job, but it does not fit in with your plans and may restrict your freedom or conflict with your ideal schedule. What do you do? This is something you should talk about with your support system.

All I can tell you is, I've come upon this point a few times in my life and I've chosen both paths, while keeping my eyes on the bigger prize. One time, I stayed the course and refused more rigid, yet profitable work, and other times, I've taken the mundane office job. It depends where you are financially, and how you're meeting your other needs like socializing, continuing your education, and/or vacation time.

Just know that time goes quickly and, if you decide to take advantage of what life throws you, then doing it for a year or two, or even five, might not get in the way of your long-term goals.

Experience can be a boon in surprising ways. I know people who have booked commercials, not because of their acting resumes, but because of their work as a server or lifeguard or experience as a long-distance runner. Sitcoms and movies have been written based on a non-industry day job the writer had.

Personally, I studied television, radio, and film production in school. Stephen Hillenburg studied marine resource planning and interpretation at Humboldt State University. (Now which one of us do you think created *Spongebob Squarepants*?)

CROWD-FUNDING

People ask for crowd-funding on individual projects but really, your entire endeavor is an individual project. Thus, you need funding. Sure, there's no guarantee your project will pay off. So, unlike a business plan you might put together to secure dinero for a retail store or online jewelry company, it's difficult to ask for financial backing for your career.

In fact, getting funding on every movie is similar. It's a gamble. That's why movies take so long to make. How can you know what will work? One person's favorite movie is another person's garbage.

Why not find capital to pursue your goal this way? Hey, it works for others. What have you got to lose? (You gotta think outside the box.)

TO MOVE ON OR NOT MOVE ON

Throughout your working life, you will find situations arise that may pose complications for you. You can say goodbye to the stifling rat race in order to free up your time to follow the reason you came to town in the first place, or you can continue taking advantage of the perks it affords you with a consistent salary.

Maybe you fell in love. Ah, l'amour! The heart can get in the way and refocus priorities. And now maybe you have a child. You need to support that child. You have your day job and you have parenting duties, so when do you work on your craft - only in the evenings when you can fit in an hour a night? Your time and crisis management skills could be put to the test.

Should you find yourself in this position, you can either double down on your goal or embrace the path you are on. There's a saying that is very popular, if not a little pie-in-the-sky optimistic, and that is, "Leap and Annette will appear!" (Now you are probably asking yourself Who the hell is Annette?! But if you say it out loud, it makes more sense -- "Leap and A NET will appear".) This means to trust that you're making the right decision. Don't look back.

QUITTING YOUR DAY JOB

Do you feel you've reached a point where you'll be able to survive on your own? Are you getting antsy at your current job? There's another popular phrase and that is, "Don't quit your day job". And there's a reason people say that; doing so at the wrong time can be irresponsible and foolish. So when is this ever a good idea?

I have known comedians who had been on television shows yet were still temping in order to pay the bills. It took a while until they were making enough from what they loved to survive solely on comedy. It depends on if your current success can fit into your work schedule and if it's enough to support you. If not, some tweaks may need to be made.

I knew that I was not long for the 9 to 5 and saved up enough money to quit, banking on finding my success before I ran out of money. It was certainly touch-and-go, but I made it. Really, it's like going to Vegas and throwing money down. Will the money make you more money or will it just disappear?

If you have no responsibilities, it's easier. I got into my path, the network track – assistant, manager, director, vice president, senior vice president, ruler of the universe – because I got a job as a page. That led me to the pool of assistants for the big wigs. But I gave up that full-time position because I wasn't happy. I much preferred my creative freedom. I was getting paid more than I had before and had benefits, but I didn't come to Hollywood for that.

I kept coming back to the stories of actors who were down to their last dimes, having packed up their cars waiting for the answer on an audition which they got from the payphone next to where they parked. The universe waits for the last possible moment just to make sure you're worthy. Are you willing to survive in a car in order to achieve your dream?

It seems silly, and I'm not sure those stories are accurate, plus how many end up living in their cars and getting a call that they *didn't* book the audition? We don't hear those stories, do we? Still, there's something romantic about it.

On the other hand, you may like your new path and see a whole new career for yourself. Staying put may not be the worst thing in the world. It's a personal decision.

CONCLUSION

Opening yourself up to a new job and a new direction also opens you up to new connections and maybe the discovery of your true passion or calling. Use your path, regardless of how random, to pick up as much knowledge and as many names as you can. Use the ones who will be helpful to you.

Go day by day, but keep your eyes on the prize. That prize can change as your mind expands, but until then, you have to juggle the needs of the present with the desires of the future.

CHAPTER 7 - MAKING A NAME FOR YOURSELF

INTRO

So you may be wondering, with the thousands of people vying for comparatively few jobs and all the flotsam and jetsam floating around there, how can you rise to the top,?

Again, you would be shocked as to what is considered exemplary work in Hollywood. Just showing up on time is viewed as impressive and a good way to endear yourself to the bosses. If people want to work with you for any of those reasons we mentioned before: talent, drive, professionalism - they will work with you. At that point, it's in the hands of fate. You still have the other talented and driven professionals with whom to contend.

DO SOMETHING

I mentioned the "big talkers" of the world, those people who *will* do so much, but never *really* do it because it's easier to talk about than to do.

You can elevate yourself above 95% of your competition by just doing *something*. It doesn't have to be perfect. (Obviously, don't show too many people if it's *that* bad, but perfection is an unrealistic goal. Use it to learn from and improve.) Show people and impress them with your ability to complete something.

If it's not the best thing out there and turns off some agents/ managers/producers, that's fine. There are many, many more people out there scouting once you improve your stuff. Each completed work is just another chance to present your stuff to get the right people to like you.

RISE THROUGH THE MINORS

Hollywood is like a baseball organization. Everyone comes to town and starts in the minor leagues. The classrooms, the performances in front of empty houses, the unread script drafts, the unheard demos all represent single-A, where lots of people have *potential*. You may be good, but still have a long way to get to the majors and lots of people to leapfrog. Just showing up gives you a better chance.

Even in the majors, there are a lot of players who are not as good as you but, as I mentioned before, focus on *your* stuff. Everyone rises to within a level above or below their individual talent grade by outside circumstances, whether beneficial or detrimental.

As you create your success at the various levels, you will see peers move at varying speeds. When I first got to town, I fell in with a group of other fresh-faced stand-ups with talent that I liked and respected. Of my original stand-up gang, or "Rookie Class", as I like to say, it played out differently for all of us:

- One went on to be a working actor and then segued into directing;
- One was a successful commercial actor who abruptly quit to become a teacher;
- One was already teaching during the day, but continued as a stand-up at night;
- One wrote a successful play and now pitches TV shows to the networks;
- Two are working writers;
- One continued to travel the country doing stand-up, while still trying to sell projects in town;
- And one went on to get a screenplay into development and write a bestselling humor book, and this one. [winky face]

Look at any improv theatre for a blueprint - you start at level 1, then rise through the ranks. Sometimes you are held back a class or two and sometimes you reach your ceiling but don't progress any further. A tiny percentage makes it to the top and then auditions for *Saturday Night Live*. That is the process throughout most of the jobs in Hollywood.

BE YOU

It's difficult to rise with so many people doing exactly what you are doing. Actors show up at casting calls to see a slew of others who look exactly like them. You'd think the final selection came down to a coin flip. (And maybe it does. You'll never know.) This seems like an obvious point, but it's not.

As an actor, you'll want to give them what you think they want. But your chances of guessing that is slim because usually they have no idea what they want until they see it, even if they *tell* you what they are looking for ahead of time. You're attempting to be the right this and the right that, so why not be the one thing you do right 100% of the time – be *you*. There's as much of a chance you're right just by being yourself.

The same goes with the other aspects of the industry, and any art really. Why play the guessing game? Why try to outdo the other "yous"? Be something they cannot and let the chips fall where they may after that. The hard part, the part that takes a while, is figuring out who you are as an artist and what exactly you bring to the table.

Many writers try to write a script because they think the topic is hot (i.e. vampire movies or whatever). *That's what the kiddies are watching these days.* By the time the script is ready, however, that market will have dried up and the public will have moved on.

Therefore, you need to write what you want to, what makes your mind leap, and your heart smile. Make it universal and timeless. Unless you get paid to write something. Then write whatever they want you to write and cash the check immediately.

Typically, if you're not jazzed by your work, it shows. Remember, there are many others who will be jazzed by the work. So how do you start getting your name out there?

BUSINESS CARDS

Literally, get your name out there. Get business cards and hand them around. Most of the time, people will take them, thank you, and then forget all about it. Or maybe they'll enter you in some giant spreadsheet. Because if they met you, they'll be meeting a bunch of other people. Before they can see that you stand out from the rest, your card must stand out. Make it a little more memorable than:

John Smith
Writer
213-525-4210

That does not do justice to your uniqueness and so why would anyone choose you over someone else?

Carry your cards with you always. You never know who you're gonna meet. That said, will it be the person who makes you famous? Not likely, but it may be the first step toward becoming successful as you never know who that person you just met knows.

Actors have been told to have postcards made which they should distribute to casting directors. These directors literally get thousands. Some will say they look at all of them, but the conventional wisdom is to send them when you have something to say, like you've booked a spot on a TV show/feature film or signed with a new agent.

Stand-ups make flyers for upcoming shows and hand them out or post them on coffee shop message boards. It usually doesn't have a big return on investment, but it looks nice to see your name there with other stand-ups. (My mother still has an early one of mine laminated in some room of her house.) I wouldn't spend too much on them. Word of mouth and online promotion are equally effective. . . and cheaper.

If you're a singer, you might want to have a demo handy, with a label or business card attached. Of course, everyone carries a smartphone or has a laptop handy now so flash drives and links may be your best bet.

Remember, don't be pushy in handing out your stuff! If someone wants to check it out, they will.

If you get a business card, send a note saying you enjoyed meeting the person. In the future, their name will automatically populate in any future e-mail correspondence and jog your memory every time you see that name. And if they respond with a note too, now your name populates in their emails.

But just waiting to hand out your card isn't enough. You have to get out there. You've ordered 500 cards. Plan to give out all of them and order your next batch.

Where can you get these cards? Literally everywhere. www.Vistaprint.com is a very popular site.

NETWORKING

Networking is the key to any business endeavor. Get names, job descriptions and connections. LA is the smallest 9 million person city in the world. Chances are, you will become connected to everyone in town within only four or five degrees.

If you have a relative, use them; if you have a friend, use him or her. That's how things get done. Talent helps, but it is not nearly the top factor for success.

But where can you network? (The better question is where *can't* you network?) There's always something going on somewhere, and though networking can bog you down in your daily quest (it's a lot of effort for very little payoff), you still have to do it. A shark never stops swimming.

More important than networking is the *perception* of networking. For those people you just want to keep in touch with, in the event that someday, they might be good to know, all you have to do is create the appearance of an interest in networking with them.

"Hey, let's get together."

"Yes! Let me look on my calendar. This week is bad, but let's talk again in a week or two."

And that will probably be all you need because, in a week or two, something has come up for one of you and the desire to get together has passed. But the *effort* was made!

Mixers

A mixer is a great place to meet industry professionals or up-and-comers such as yourself. Don't spend your entire time talking with one person. Just chat with them long enough to get a sense of who the person is and what kind of connection you might have with them (i.e., you both are from Milwaukee, you both like to ski, you both love sci-fi, etc.). And find a mutual benefit either socially or professionally (but mainly professionally).

Once the event is over, it's up to you to keep the relationship going. Once you leave that place, they're off to meet other people and you just blend into the crowd . . . unless you *stood out*.

Panels

You'll want to attend panel discussions aimed at your vocation. There you can meet more peers, but mainly it's about engaging the experts, those who impart advice. And if you ever meet them again, you can bring up the time that you met them.

At many of these panels, you will hear people ask the questions you want answered. These generally follow a recurring theme:

- How does one break in?
- Should I get an agent?
- How do you get an agent?
- How do I know when I'm ready?
- How did you break in?
- How do what do should do do dooo? Blah blah blah.

The point is, you'll get lots of direct, *definitive* answers which don't help you at all. Because your path is going to be unique. And many of these questions are not the right questions to ask.

One thing people believe is that you need an agent or a manager to succeed. But many times, the way you get an agent or manager is actually *by* succeeding. This is the original catch-22.

Agents connect you. If you already have the connections you need, then you don't need an agent. A lawyer, yes, as you want someone trained to look over contracts.

The truth is, yes, people get agents who, in turn, help them get their first jobs. But also, people become successful through another conduit and then have representatives offering to take them on as clients to help them break through to the *next* level and parlay that first success into more. That seems more likely, for it is rare that someone takes a chance on an unproven commodity, even when many declare they are taking on new talent.

And the question about breaking in – panelists will tell you what they've seen. If they are writers or producers, they'll say a "production assistant" is the right entry-level position. It's good, it's non-specific, and it provides an opportunity to meet people that they know. But it doesn't guarantee anything. You can have a job as a PA, have it lead to nothing, but feel like you're doing something. Or you could not get a job as a PA and still progress to where you want to be somehow, but that's not specific and no one can tell you exactly what to do then.

If they are actors, they will tell you to keep acting. That's nice, and probably good advice, but forget about it and just do what you do. Every story is different, as yours will be.

The panels are inspiring though. These are living, breathing people who have made it to where you want to go.

So when you leave the panel, you feel energized, like you have a direction. But you are still on your own to forge your own path.

THE NETWORKING HANDSHAKE

One funny thing I've observed at networking events is the schmoozer. This is the person who likes to employ what I call the "networking handshake".

Take one hand and extend it while maintaining a broad smile and eye contact. Once a connection has been made, most likely in the form of a handshake pulling into a chest bump and optional "dap" (i.e. pat on the back after chest contact has been made), you can lose the eye contact. At this point, you've accomplished your mission and reconnected. Now, you have to find the next person to talk to even as you're still talking to this guy. *Hey, great to see you! You look great! We should definitely get together and grab lunch!* And you've already moved on.

Basically, you pull someone in and look around the room as you shake his hand to see if you find anyone more important you need to talk to. It's a status thing. Women can do it with a polite hug or cheek to cheek kiss.

COMPLEMENT YOUR SUPPORT SYSTEM

You need to be smart about those you add to your support system. It's good to know everyone, but you only have so much time in your life and space in your brain. Therefore, look to complement it.

If you meet someone in the same boat as you (*I'm a writer and love improv!* "Me too!"), decide if you need another peer. It comes down to asking yourself whether they have something to offer your career, or just in life. Maybe they run in the same circles as you, maybe they have a connection you'd like.

It doesn't have to be completely superficial. You may genuinely enjoy that person and want to socialize with them as much as do business. But when? We'll talk about rotating your connections while maintaining a social life in Chapter 10.

Facebook definitely helps you stay connected. If you meet someone and connect via Facebook, you can continue getting to know them through their posts, albeit through a voyeuristic lens. (*Oh, this person and I both like that movie* or *She's been to Peru also* or *He/She is funny.)* That's how networking is just the beginning. Keep them at the ready.

USING YOUR CONNECTIONS

You don't always have to leave the house to network. Using your connections (i.e. friends, family, etc.) and their network can work faster. Really, networking can be done anywhere. I once met a lady on a train who wanted to help and knew this "very successful literary agent" so I got her to make an introduction.

When asking for help from your contacts, there's a 3-step process:

1. Have your contact ask his/her connection on your behalf.

   Andy, ol' buddy,

   My good friend, Rick, who you met before, has a daughter, Katie, who is in New York City and has been scraping by (sound familiar?) making a living in comedy, performing with an improv troupe, waitressing, etc. She was home the other day visiting family and expressed an interest in moving to LA. I told her she HAD to contact you. I know you are busy, but would that be possible? If you have the time, could you answer any questions she may have? It would be appreciated.

   Signed, Bob

2. Once you have the go ahead, write a polite note reiterating your connection, how little time you'd like to take up, a brief summary of your goals, and a question or two you're looking to have answered.

   Hi, Andy,

   Bob recommended I give you a call. He said you're the man to know. I really appreciate you letting me pick your brain. As he mentioned, I am moving to LA and was just wondering what the first step to take is. If you could give me ten minutes of your time, that'd be great. Thanks.

   Signed, Katie

Most of the time, the person will give you more time than you ask for, but keep your request short. Or, if you are looking to follow up with a panelist that you met at one of the events, you can accomplish this with a simple, *"I met you at so-and-so and was wondering if this-and-that . . ."*

3. Have the conversation and, when it is done, send a nice, brief note, thanking your beneficiary. If you do this over the phone, you can decide if you were grateful enough at the end of the conversation, but if all questions were answered via e-mail or letter, then yes, you need to send a thank you, even via e-mail. It's on you to end the charitable deed with graciousness.

Not doing that reflects poorly on both you and the person who connected you.

COVER LETTERS

You will probably send a lot of letters cold, that is, without a referral or previous introduction. Whether you are querying an agent as an actor, potential employer as an editor, production company as a writer, or looking for information as a fresh-faced grad, it is important to understand what makes a good cover letter.

First, you need to compile a list of people that might have a need for your talents. (If it's only one person that you are pinpointing, then that's fine too.)

Use the Internet, references from friends, social networking, buy the latest version of the Hollywood Screenwriting Directory, or even call the company for basic information (chat up an assistant or receptionist).

If you are pitching a script, do not call and say, *"Have I got an idea for you!"* That's gonna get you a big "n-o" right there. Hold onto your idea until you've made contact, or at least enticed the person with your well-thought out cover letter.

On average, if you are sending out mass emails/letters, you'll hit on about 5-10% of them. These people are paid to scout to see what's out there in the vast sea of material and artists. You'll know soon whose curiosity you've piqued. If there's interest, then you can follow up. Most of the time, you'll never hear from them again. Their e-mail address still works. It's just that they were not interested.

Most places in town receive tons upon tons of query letters and enough headshots to replenish the Amazon rainforest. If you've read in an industry book that this company or this person accepts unsolicited submissions, then by all means, give it a shot. They are searching for you, but you've got to stand out without being too crazy. That is, stay within the parameters of the format and let the content of your letter and *not* its style speak for itself.

Here is your cover letter tutorial:

1. If you have a referral, mention that up front, or in the subject line if you are e-mailing. It puts you ahead of 99% of the other letters. If you don't have a referral, just put something about you that will entice them, such as "Bestselling Author with Science Fiction Script" or "Julliard-trained Actor Looking for Rep" or "George Clooney Recommended that I Contact You" (only if he did, in fact, recommend this).
2. Keep it short and to the point. They are not looking for flowery literature.
3. Don't try to be too funny or creative. Leave that for your links or Twitter feed that you list under your signature.
4. List your most unique traits, anything that you think will encourage interest in your bio, which is usually your first paragraph (*I'm a* _____ *who is looking for a* _____ *. . .*) or the second to last paragraph (*A little something about me . . .*) after you've already put your pitch out there.
5. Four paragraphs total, and not more than two concise sentences in each. If you need to use a series to list your accomplishments, then choose three to four of your most impressive. And I always find bullet points to be more eye-catching.
6. Remember to personalize it to some degree. If it looks like a form letter going out, you're less likely to find success.

To summarize, it's:

- Referral/greeting explaining who you are and what you want
- What you bring to the table/logline of idea
- Brief bio
- "I look forward to hearing from you."

If your purpose is just informational in scope, then it may be okay to cold call, but sometimes it's best to spell out your motives and needs first in a letter. Then, you can set up a time that the two parties can speak when they will have fewer distractions.

In terms of a follow up after your *initial* follow up, I'd say two to three weeks is good. People love to make contact right away just to see what you've got. Then, the interest may wane once they *see* what you've got. Or they have to dedicate more focus and attention to your cause as they consider your qualifications and potential. You never know. But like anything else in town, if you continue to hear nothing, move on.

TAKING MEETINGS

Better than talking over the phone, people love to talk in person, whether in an office or in the informal lunch/coffee setting. People love to take meetings. In fact, LA is (unofficially) the "meeting capital of the world".

People take meetings a lot. "Let's do lunch," is a popular phrase, almost as popular as "Sorry I'm late, but traffic . . ." (Though those exact words may not be used, the idea is, you're going to spend a lot of time just *talking* about things.)

Two things a meeting does: (a) it gets you excited. Something is happening. You're talking about the future, and preparing for something, something that could be big. Creative juices are flowing. I imagine that creative juices are similar to endorphins, only you're sitting at the time and not risking a torn ACL.

And (b) it makes it seem like things are moving. (Again, in a "hurry up and wait" culture, just keeping busy is refreshing and necessary.)

There are always so many balls in the air that, as excited as you are or someone else is about your meeting, there are other meetings each player is excited for, too. A co-producer on a project calls me and gives me the full rundown on where we are and what he's going to do next on my project. "I'm on it," he says. Then he tells me of the six other projects that he's "on".

There's a mentality of "throw enough against the wall and something will stick". (My mother made me think she invented that phrase and got a royalty every time she used it.)

Imagine those plate spinners. You try to keep the plates spinning all at once. Take as many meetings as you can. And in the interim, keep doing more things so, when you meet people, you can tell them all what you are doing. The key to this is remaining focused on your craft.

A corporation does the same. Executives run from meeting to meeting. One might wonder what they ever get done since they're always in meetings. They may never get anything done other than overseeing all the meetings, but eventually they produce results.

You are your own corporation. You have to meet, but during the other moments, you have to work – practice your scenes, write your pieces, compile your team to produce your series, etc.

When one of two types of meetings comes up, you'll be ready.

Project Meetings

First, there are meetings with a purpose. You're talking about that idea that's going to happen or may happen or you would like to happen and what needs to be done to get it to happen. Go to any coffee shop and you'll witness one of these discussions.

If you're called into an office for such a meeting, they already know you're pretty good (or at least a qualified candidate on their short list), so don't stress. Don't show up in a tank top and flip flops, but just be cool. Whatever they are meeting you about, this could someday be your job, so treat it like your day-to-day existence. Remind yourself you deserve to be there. Arrive on time. (Remember traffic and consider the time it takes to park and walk somewhere, especially if your meeting is on one of the studio lots.)

Just talking about your ideas or projects can get you jazzed. So can watching quality finished projects. It may be why you became an actor in the first place, because you saw *Rent* on Broadway, or used to read *People* magazine. This stuff is like catnip to the creative feline.

The projects may not pan out (very few do), but without meetings, you've never even given them a shot.

Informational Meetings

Informational meetings are different, but still important. You may finally get called in and stress out as it's a big deal to you but, to them, it's just a chance to get to know you. Imagine you are going to lunch with your co-workers. Be engaging and honest.

These meetings represent a good first step, like that networking event, only in a more subdued and personal environment where the focus is on you. (And them. Don't be afraid to ask questions, too.)

Lots of times, you'll leave thinking how great it went. And that's good that you didn't piss anyone off or it didn't have the feel of a funeral. You are now allowed to remain "on the list". But if there's no specific project to attach your talents to, then there's nothing more you can hope for at that time.

With any luck, this will lead to something in the future.

CONTESTS/FELLOWSHIPS/FESTIVALS

These are huge for scriptwriters and filmmakers more than anyone else. (Actors and the rest of the creative team on these projects also gain exposure.) Get your work out there! If you can't meet anyone in person, use this avenue to work your way in front of them. Contests are sponsored to find the cream of the undiscovered crop.

Getting your script chosen is like throwing a wet dart at a moving board. Writing fellowships can help you rise faster but, if not, you are not to get discouraged. There are so many variables that you run into:

- Do the judges have the same sense of humor as me?
- Is the judge tired at the time of reading my script?
- Is the film their cup of tea?
- Is the judge a failed and bitter writer themselves?
- Has the judge seen the show you are presenting to them in a spec script?

Remember that the whole industry is subjective and you don't know who's judging you so take every rejection or every acceptance with a grain of salt.

I received a note once from a reader at a prominent film festival who said he wanted to see "more of the guest star". What is the first rule you learn for writing spec scripts? Keep the guest star to a minimum. The guest star is a character you make up and no one is reading your spec script (of an existing show) to see how you write new characters. A spec is to highlight how well you write *existing* characters.

So it was clear that this reader did not have a good grasp on the rules of sitcom writing. Yet this was the person put in charge of selecting those scripts that would advance. Oooof!

Put another way, it's like going to the doctor and receiving a diagnosis of heartburn when there's a pitchfork jutting out of your chest.

> *"Who said you could be a doctor?"*
> *"Well, we were a little short-staffed and I'm a big fan of*
> *Grey's Anatomy."*

From the contests that I've judged, I can say you'll always find that the majority of scripts/films are pretty good, a couple are fantastic, and a couple should be burned with a nuclear-grade liquid.

Actors also have opportunities to be seen. Send your demo to agents or network showcases. It's *American Idol* without the Internet voting or without the Seacrest. And stand-ups need to have their tightest sets (or best bits) loaded online at all times.

It's still the same thing. This just proves that you're putting all your diligence, training, and experience into the hands of people who may have no training, diligence, or experience, but want to feel they're contributing to your discovery in some way.

Still, for the benefits they may provide, and the small financial burden, these opportunities may be your best way to step closer. I've won contests and had nothing happen yet also found success after losing contests.

CONCLUSION

You are a corporation. First order of business, advertise your start up to the world. You have a good product (you), but need to promote it. Unless you have the funds, you must handle your own marketing, public relations, social media interaction, etc. During daylight hours (and potentially when others sleep), you need to cultivate this business.

Very few people rise to the majors in a day (Ken Griffey Jr. is the exception) and most companies toil in anonymity before hitting the New York Stock Exchange.

Dan Brown had no one show up at his Barnes & Noble signing for *The Da Vinci Code* until his book found its way into Oprah's hands. Short of having ties to Oprah, you've gotta work all your angles to get to that point. That means using your entire network and meeting as many people as you can. Keep this in mind as you play all your chips, for you never know which will be the lucky one that propels you further along your path.

You will meet people by attracting them to the work you are doing. Then you will see who is as competent and committed as you are and who is just blowing smoke or blissfully unqualified.

Find success by succeeding. Do it yourself because when you are waiting for others to help with your project, you'll just be left waiting.

CHAPTER 8 - KNOWING THE CODE

INTRO

This may be the most important chapter of all. It's the stuff everyone who lives in Hollywood knows, but doesn't discuss. It pulls back the curtain on the Wizard.

Before you move out here, you're told very little about the culture of LA. You'll assume it's just like everywhere else – get up, put your pants on one leg at a time, and hit it. Not quite. For the industry is a game and, as in every game, there are quirky rules, i.e. "Do not pass go, do not collect $200." LA is no different. It's understanding these rules and subsequently thriving in the culture that represents the difference between swimming and drowning.

You won't find this stuff on Google translator, so take notes!

HOLLYWOOD TIME

Everyone is late. It's probably because of traffic, but usually isn't. It's because people put less of a priority on promptness than they do on clothing.

Let's say a party is arranged for 8 p.m. You can be fashionably late, maybe a half hour, or closer to an hour. But in Hollywood, it would not surprise anyone if you went by "Hollywood time". An 8 o'clock party can be joined around 10 or 11. If you have something to do ahead of time, great. If not, you can still show up late to give the appearance you had something else to do ahead of time.

I was invited to a small New Year's Eve party recently and showed up a half hour late. I was alone with the hosts for almost 90 minutes. That's indicative of what you can expect. Now, does that mean you show up two hours late to every party? No, but if you did, it would not seem as out of place as my "early" arrival, unfortunately.

Another friend of mine, a guy living with two girls, once had a *Three's Company* party. (Get it? A guy with two girls.) One of his roommates worked at NBC where she had contact with Richard Kline, the actor who played Larry Dallas on the iconic sitcom. Word went out to Richard about the party and he showed up a few minutes after the party started, to the delight of . . . the three people who lived there. So it was him and the hosts for a while, until he left to attend another party . . . shortly before any other guests arrived.

THE "SILENT NO"

I was interviewed for a job to be the personal assistant of a big star on a show when I first got to town. The associate producer called to tell me I just didn't have enough experience dealing with celebrities, so they went with someone else. This was fine with me. I had no experience, so I didn't expect anything. I appreciated how she was so open and honest. No big whoop.

My first interview in the industry job world resulted in a rejection call. I figured that was how the real world operated, and rightfully so. It was courteous and professional. Alas, it was the very *last* time I have ever received a call telling me negative news. It's just not done here. Maybe the associate producer was new at her job, maybe she was new in town and not familiar with the Hollywood code of conduct. (Either way, she was very sweet and completely out of place.)

I'm sure there are people who will get defensive and flip out when bad news is relayed (that's life), but you should still be dignified when hearing a "no", whether it be by e-mail, smoke signal, carrier pigeon, etc. A cold, standardized and impersonal e-mail is even better than no reply at all.

Without calling anyone back, employing the tiniest shred of common courtesy, you risk running into the person again in this small town and perhaps needing something from them. You never know.

I'm glad I got the rejection call because it gave me a chance to ask about other job openings. She put me on hold and, as luck would have it, there was a production assistant there who mentioned the network's page program. The next day, I applied for that and got in to the network that way.

She and I crossed paths several times at the office (thanks to my all-access page pass) and I always thanked her for her kindness. The reunion would have been more awkward had she blown me off initially.

It's called the "silent no" and is a part of the self-preservation mentality here. It comes down to people being afraid to hurt other people's feelings. If anyone rejects you, they know a) they might be turning down something that turns out to be the "next big thing" and they don't want that on their conscience so they just never turn it down, b) they know that people keep a shit list and they don't want to contribute their name to it (of course, a "silent no" is grounds for inclusion on any such list), and c) you can't be passive and laid back when you are direct and professional.

This is what you have to get used to in Hollywood – no callbacks, replies, kept promises, and so on. The stuff that happens – you'd swear even sixth-graders knew better. These are working adults. Ah, yes, but they're Hollywood adults. (In other words, not quite up to a sixth-grade level of maturity yet.)

So when is a reasonable time to follow up? As I mentioned in the previous chapter, two weeks is good (unless you were given a specific day by which to have an answer). And then, if you don't receive any reply, another week. If you're getting the brush off, you can e-mail or call every day, and it won't hurt your standing (heck, they already think very little of you), but there's an unspoken rule that you should know you're being blown off.

It's like dating. If you keep pushing, you look desperate. Spend your time going after someone who wants you. This is what people who blow off other people bank on.

POSTPONING MEETINGS

More people in this industry get "sick" when you've set up a meeting. If you are meeting with someone and that meeting has no immediate discernible business advantages, expect them to get "sick". There are times when people legitimately come down with something (after all, many people burn the candle at both ends), but if you were important, they'd "take some Pepto Bismol and come on over", to quote Ferris Bueller.

There's actually a hierarchy; if someone needs you more than you need them (or you outrank them), then you can play the "cancel card". If you're equal, you can each pull the card once, but only if something more important comes up. That is to say, if you are canceled on, then you can cancel once before meeting.

If you are inferior (I'm speaking in terms of professional status here), do not cancel, and do not bank on that meeting taking place as scheduled.

KNOW THIS: Never cancel up.

My boss, a network veep, once asked if she had previously canceled on the man she was having lunch with. I told her she hadn't, so she said, "Call him and reschedule then."

What you would logically expect elsewhere is not to be expected here, without first consulting your Berlitz book on English-to-Hollywood speak.

A DIFFERENT LANGUAGE

Los Angeles is a town of many different tongues, from English and Tagalong to Spanish and Chinese. But there are words and terms that fit into none of these, words you thought you understood, only to find that here, they mean something totally different. Once you learn these words and phrases, you'll be better off.

"Definitely"

Certainly words like "definitely" take on a different meeting. See if you can spot the slight variation between the two phrases:

> *We'll get together soon.*
> *We'll definitely get together soon.*

On the surface, both phrases mean the two parties will soon be hanging out together. And in a normal town, the word implies an assurance. But in Hollywood, once someone adds the term "definitely", it creates the inverse effect. They will not be hanging out.

We'll definitely get together soon provides the appearance of excitement and motivation, but actually has the opposite effect. It means *"My excitement should be enough of an effort to inform you of my desire without actually having to take time out of my schedule to follow through."*

Many times this is done after running into someone and briefly catching up. *"It was great seeing you. We should do something more formal, like a lunch."* "Definitely", i.e. "It seems unnecessary since we've already caught up with each other."

It's an odd phenomenon. Do not take it personally.

"We should get together"

This is said when someone needs something from you. The phrase makes it sound like you both have something to gain by meeting. *We should? Well, why wasn't I made aware of that?!* That's usually what you think. But what you say is, "Oh, yeah, definitely!" The phrase is code for "I feel like I want to hang out with you, but it's not a top priority right now."

"I'll call you later today"

This phrase is shorthand for "I won't call you later today". You may find it odd that the contraction "I'll" is used in place of "I won't", but you shouldn't. Shorthand doesn't need to be accurate; it just needs to be shorter.

"I'll get to it this weekend"

This means, "It'll be at least another month before I get to it". No one is ever too busy if the project is important enough. It's just a matter of prioritizing.

If they haven't already done so, they will not be doing it that weekend as there are other things that take precedence in their lives, whether it be business or pleasure.

Saying this prepares you for the idea that it is getting close to the time it will be done. Keep on trying them until they wear down and finally get to it or just stop lying to you about when they'll get it done.

"A.S.A.P."

"As soon as possible," right? WRONG! These letters literally have no connection to one another. They are gibberish in this town. But people love to throw it around as if they know how to use it in context.

I love the idea! I love the world! I love the characters! Let me read it and I'll get back to you A.S.A.P.

Those were the exact words from a big-time actor/ director to my co-producer in a meeting he took on a project I'd written. "He's such a nice guy, no ego at all," my producer assured me. Now, I didn't want to be cynical, but a tiny little piece of me said, "Well, he IS an actor." (He could be *acting* like he had no ego.)

Two weeks go by. Nothing. A follow up email to his company. Nothing. Ah, the "silent no".

"A.S.A.P." sounds nice to say, very official and authoritative, but it's useless. Again, it's funny to see how people can go to great lengths to be polite and complimentary only to make themselves out to be bigger jerks.

"Next week"

Everything will happen next week (or *this* week, whatever, doesn't matter). When next week comes, it'll still happen *next* week. Similar to "I'll get to it this weekend," the literal translation is somewhere between one to two months.

"You'll never work in this town again!"

If this is ever said to you, don't worry. The person saying it is literally a crazy person, clinging to any perception of power they think they have. Anyone who does have the power to crush you will just do it with a snap of their fingers or by using the Force to choke you to death.

I was doing a stand-up show once. I received a text from the comedian booking me. "How many people do you have coming tonight?"

"I don't know," I replied. "I have seven maybes." (Which in LA is at least five nos.)

"I need to know!" he texted.

"I can't tell you exactly. Between zero and seven." I was being honest, but also polite. What did he want me to do, kidnap my friends' dogs until they promised to come to my show?

He went into how his is an exclusive show (it wasn't), how top agents and managers were coming (they didn't), and how it was comedians like me who gave the craft a bad name. (The irony in that statement from him was not lost on me, of course. The "craft" of comedy has nothing to do with inviting guests to attend the show.) Then, he dropped the "I'll tell everyone in town to never book you again" line.

I thanked him and told him it was nice to be talked about.

The funny thing was, after his incendiary texts, he didn't delete me from his mass text list (sent to all available comedians for his "exclusive" show) and I continued to receive requests for shows from him until I simply texted back "unsubscribe".

"Confirmed"

This is one of those words that just represents a bold-faced lie. Yes, it happens, with no qualms, by agents, executives, those types of people; cold, unfeeling people who, through a fear of losing their current lives and status, will stomp on anyone and wake up the next day with no understanding of their actions. They're like Godzilla. That said, they can help you. You want them on your side. So smile when you meet one and forget everything I've ever said about them.

I was involved in a project with a producer from a very popular Comedy Central show, a show that featured many celebrity guest stars. The casting director of that show reached out to the agent of an actor we wanted. After a brief back and forth, the agent asked for an offer, which we made. And then we got the word – "He's confirmed. We're just trying to pick out a date."

So the producer moved forward to set up locations, get a crew, dot the i's and cross the t's, and the casting director went forward to cast the second lead opposite this "confirmed" actor.

A follow up call to said agent a week or so later for the date found a slightly different tone – "Well, he's never read the script and neither have I. I never said he was confirmed." (Actually, those were your exact words.) "How about if you write a note saying what the project's about and why he should do it?"

So I wrote a note describing in four paragraphs essentially what the four-page script would have told him. In fact, it probably would've taken either of them less time to read the script than to read the letter. It was inane and made no sense, especially for an actor who was now only doing small guest spots.

This one day shoot for $1500 (more than actor's scale) would have been a benefit to him if the project succeeded. It was a win-win, but as we know, agents are not the most forthright people.

Until the production is shot and edited or the check is in your bank account and has cleared, nothing is confirmed.

Math Discrepancies

Numbers are not calibrated either. If someone says, *"It's 99.9% gonna get picked up,"* that's about 50% give or take a tick or two. You'd be surprised how large a number like .1% is in Hollywood. It's much larger than those nerdy mathematicians on the outside ever imagined.

FACEBOOK/TWITTER ANNOUNCEMENTS

Social media makes things easier, from keeping in touch to promoting yourself. In fact, it's now just as important to promote yourself.

Consider this: agents and managers used to have to take the time to read full scripts. That was the only way they knew if you were a good writer or not. Or they could cut down on that commitment and see a play, or they could read something shorter like a funny limerick. And for actors and stand-ups, they needed to take the time to pop a videotape into the machine and sit through five minutes or so. Everyone has always sought to spend as little time as possible doing something.

Enter technology! Nowadays, they can click on a link you've posted of a project you've completed. But even that might take three minutes. So better yet, they can read 140 characters of a tweet. That's time-efficiency! No more of these two to three rambling paragraphs in a cover letter.

Every time you post on Facebook and Twitter, imagine that you are auditioning for your job. If you feel you're going to be political or edgy, and that's *not* your thing professionally, then keep two homepages. Make sure the side you want people to see has more friends or followers.

Lots of people just check your numbers to see how many people follow you. Even if you can't get 7 million subscribers on your YouTube channel, you may still be a commodity. Several thousand on Twitter is solid. Ten thousand gets you all the respect you need. Two to three hundred, meh, notsomuch. One good rule is to make sure you have more followers than people you follow. This is a weird validation thing, as if this means you are a bigger player than you are.

Not too adept at social media? There are now companies where you can buy followers and retweets to enhance your numbers. Yes, that's right! Even social media has performance-enhancing drugs. (Yes, it's morally dubious, but in Hollywood, they don't care how you got them, just that you have them.) Just keep up your activity to make your follower count believable.

Keep in mind, there are rules to tweeting. Some of these rules get by even the most professional people (i.e. sports heroes who show how racist, sexist, or homophobic they are) or politicians who say stupid things, making you consider how dumb the constituents who follow them must be. They receive blowback and then have to claim their accounts were hacked and remove the offending tweet. And then they go on as if nothing has happened once the news cycle transitions.

As an up-and-comer, you will not be so lucky, so you must be careful. A lot of it comes from your need to promote yourself. You post that you just filmed a commercial or whatever, and then you find out the company (which heavily promotes themselves and asks you to do the same) gets mad at you because they weren't ready to announce anything yet. Or you are happy you have a booked an audition and post about it online. MY GOD!!! WHAT HAVE YOU DONE?!

Say you post a status update about having to work late on the set one night; not upset, but matter-of-fact: typical, innocuous stuff. But if your boss sees it. . . uh oh! Hollywood is hypersensitive to this stuff and you might find your contract is not renewed and you won't know why. People in Hollywood are paranoid, so this World Wide Web thing freaks them out, as does everything else.

Then, there's the fandom stuff. You got to attend a taping of a production as a friend of the producer and posted a photo of the guest actor. Everyone who was there in the audience knows the guest actor who is on the show, but you posted it on Twitter without permission from someone important because it was not yet public knowledge or for some other silly reason. There's a lot of money at stake and though they may be at fault (how were you supposed to know?), it's easier to blame you for *their* mistakes.

KNOW THIS: A simple rule of thumb is if you don't *need* to post it, don't post it.

As a final note on social media, you should follow everyone in your desired field. There are some wonderful people on Facebook.

Many will post motivational stuff which helps keep you inspired to go out and battle every day. But others are looking for a creative outlet, one that is not being recognized by the Hollywood machine. And they are hilarious!

Again, it's now become a place where you can try out stuff and be discovered. So promote your hopes, your dreams, your experiences, and your achievements with fervor, but always know when NOT to promote.

CONCLUSION

The unwritten rules are illogical, wacky, counterintuitive, useless, annoying, and totally adhered to. That's Hollywood for you. Many have tried to change them, but to no avail. The motto here is, "If you don't like it, leave."

The best thing you can do is learn to deal with it. What's said to you and what's meant probably aren't the same. Knowing this will save you lots of waking hours getting your hopes up and increasing your anger when someone doesn't follow through on what was promised.

CHAPTER 9 - SUPPORTING YOUR FRIENDS

INTRO

One thing that Los Angeles never lacks is the chance to see your friends perform live: stand-up, plays, one man shows, etc. As an artist, you need your supporters to support you . . . and in return, they need your support for all their artistic endeavors. Friends will ask you to see their performances, read the scripts they write, visit their art exhibits, or listen to their demos, ALL. . . THE. . . TIME.

It's a constant barrage of *Read my script, see my show, can you give me feedback on. . .?* As if this generation wasn't already inundated with enough stimuli.

GIVE AND TAKE

In order to keep the pipeline of audience members flowing, an artist needs to have many non-artist friends. But for many performers, your community, your workplace is typically the stage, so most of the people you know are other artists. Artists are not the wealthiest people in the world either, so don't expect any of these friends to buy your wares, whether it be a book or DVD or whatever, regardless of how much they want to support you financially. But they can easily provide moral support . . . time permitting.

If they buy something of yours or donate to a campaign, then it would be polite to do the same for them. But don't feel obligated. Especially because all things are not created equal nor do they cost the same. And what's the point? You get money from them and then give it right back.

You also don't want to spend all your time attending their shows or reading their works. You have your own work to do. But you do want to keep the give-and-take alive. If they don't feel the same way, you can jettison them from your network and it will be a burden lifted, freeing you from acts of kindness. You'll have many other people requiring your time, after all.

It's always nice to support them, of course, but it can put you into a tricky spot – the review.

YOUR REVIEW

The post mortem, that time after watching a performance or reading a script and your friend asks, "So what'd you think?"

After a Performance

The show has already happened, so any constructive criticism is useless, unless it's a performance that is going to be tweaked. And the performer obviously doesn't want to feel like a failure, so you have to tread carefully.

After attending a performance, as a rule, your answer should be, "The show was great; you were fantastic!" If you are being honest, this will come off naturally, but if you found nothing redeeming, then your answer is, "The show was good; you were *great*". (Yes, they were still "great".) Stick to the script and do not spend too much time on this. Get in, get out. (Unless you want to alienate this friend, then tell them every little flaw, drop the mic, and walk away forever.)

If you start breaking down elements of the performance, you're doomed. Actors spend so much time in their heads anyway that this could literally make their heads explode. (Yes! LITERALLY! I've seen it happen. . . Okay, it was in a movie, but he *was* an actor!)

Remember, it's all subjective. No one knows anything, so what's the point of giving an opinion you believe, that in the grand scheme of things, may not amount to anything? Your garbage may be another's award-winning production.

Case in point: The first stand-up showcase I did featured five comedians, including one who has become one of the biggest comedy names out there today. It would not be an understatement to say that this comedian was so horrendous that the audience was pretty offended by the material. Of course, there's a market for lowbrow, offensive material, and this person tapped into it in spades.

My friend Don had a unique plan on how to deal with the post mortem. Before he watched me perform for the first time, he told me ahead of the show that, regardless of what he thought, he was not going to comment. It was great foresight on his part because he didn't want to be caught lying if he thought I was bad or sounding as if he was just saying I was good if he thought I was good.

Then, afterwards, he gushed with compliments and told me he had only said that before the show to save the awkward moment. This cannot be understated! Had he only known the standardized response, it would have been easier for him. (But I appreciate him as an open and honest friend . . . one who sticks out like a sore thumb in Hollywood, an oasis in the Phony Desert.)

It's a policy I wish I had known during one late night in New York City. I was hanging out with Jason, a stand-up comedy friend. He let me stay in his apartment and joined me when I told him I had a high school friend who wanted to get together. My high school friend, Matt, was a high-energy, late-night guy who took us early-to-bed stand-ups (I know, not exactly conducive to the profession) around town from the bars to a pool hall.

Finally, we returned to Matt's place sometime after two in the morning. Jason was polite enough to join us, but he was exhausted. In fact, we were both ready to go home but, before we could exit, Matt explained he had just ventured onto the stand-up stage for the first time a month earlier and wanted my HONEST opinion of his set.

In spite of the lateness of the hour, we sat down and watched his five minute set. Now, at the time, I'd been performing stand-up about five years compared to his five *times*, so I felt it was acceptable to expect growing pains.

When the set ended, I gave him notes, beginning with the positive: "You are much more comfortable on stage than I was my first few times." And then providing him with some gentle, constructive criticism.

For each criticism, he defended himself, which is a natural reaction to criticism. *You clearly don't know what was going through my head at the time and that makes your take on my performance wrong.* (As any creative will understand at some point in their career, if you have to explain yourself to one person, it probably isn't going to work, since it's impossible to explain your motives to an entire audience.)

I rephrased my criticism once, then twice, trying to remain helpful while addressing his concerns. Finally, after a few minutes of this Mexican stand-off, Matt turns to Jason and asks succinctly, "What'd *you* think?"

"I thought it was great," he replied, without batting an eye. Within two minutes, we were out the door and heading back to Jason's apartment. I had learned my lesson regarding criticism.

KNOW THIS: Some people ask for criticism when all they really want is validation.

Script Notes

Imagine a doctor's predicament. His/her friends and family are constantly peppering him with medical questions. Though it may be annoying, this doctor can typically answer all questions with a verbal response or pass it off to another doctor through a referral rather quickly. *"Sounds like you have the flu. See this doctor. He's/She's the best in his/her field. Tell him I sent you . . . Now get out of my line of sight so I can sink this putt."*

On the other hand, if you are a script writer or any creative type, really, you will have lots of friends asking you to read their scripts. And a script is nothing you can pass judgement on in two minutes. That's a commitment of a couple of hours, at *least*. If it's particularly bad or you can see it's going nowhere, you can start skimming, or skip some pages, or just stop reading altogether and give notes. Heck, if you went to high school, you're probably familiar with the technique. (It's how I "read" *The Grapes of Wrath* and *Ethan Frome*.)

In fact, readers and execs for entertainment companies are known for their shortcuts like reading the first ten pages only, or if that's too much, the first and last pages.

There are some ways to provide your opinion without offending or sounding confrontational. Some tips to reviewing scripts:

1. Always start with the positive
   How do you navigate such a dilemma, you ask?
   Focus on something positive and be vague about it.

Avoid specifics. *It's funny! I laughed out loud many times.* (This is probably not the best tact for a drama.) *Really great concept/I can see it on the screen/These movies are in right now, so your timing is good.* (Typically, though if you are reading a script that mirrors what's on the screen currently, it won't be by the time your script actually comes to life, which can take years.)

There are some great moments/set pieces in this. (Of course, have one example handy. They usually won't call you on more than one.)

Just go with it. *What did you like about it?* "I liked this part." *What about that part did you like?* "It really made me think." Blah blah blah, you get the picture.

2. Don't just criticize, but come up with a solution

It could simply be a general idea of where to go with it, you don't need to rewrite the damn thing. *I think the lead character should have something that provides an obstacle to his goal, like a ruthless boss, or a conniving ex-brother-in-law.*

Anyone can throw out negatives. Be helpful, even if you're not *really* being helpful.

3. Never qualify the writer's efforts

Don't say, "*This is a good start*" or "*It's fine. . . for a first draft.*" It may very well be their *twentieth* draft. And perhaps they've paid for consultants to help them, too. This reflects poorly on you rather than their draft, as it comes off as condescending.

4. Be honest, but gentle

Even if it needs a page one rewrite, use the phrase, "*It just needs a little tweaking,*" or "*The main framework is there. You're on your way!*" or "*You're almost there*" also help immensely. You can bend the language in order to make it gentle.

5. Eliminate words like "few" and "major" from your critique

There are a few major issues you need to correct can be relayed the same way with *There are a couple of issues to*

correct. The fact that his main character develops superpowers and then inexplicably loses them is not a huge problem. It's easily fixable, mainly by not having the main character develop superpowers and then inexplicably lose them.

If large issues, structural or integral plot points, are seen as small, or as merely larg*er*, they are easier to deal with.

6. Keep the hyperbole to a minimum
    "This is the greatest script I've read in a long time/I wish I had written this script/It's so good, I want to punch you." You don't want to get their hopes up, do you?

7. Ask for their opinion. Many times, they'll answer their own questions and you can reiterate what they believe.

Clearly, you are welcome to follow this protocol should the script be great, but those times just call for reinforcement, and honesty. *"I think it's great"* works when you genuinely believe that as well. (Though you might want to add *". . . and I'm not just saying that"* in the event they have read this book and become irrevocably cynical.)

Remember, as much as you know, you know nothing. Because there may be someone, somewhere who feels the script can be fixed and is willing to pay your friend for his terrible idea. People with money are bigger wild cards than people with power. A financier might *love* scripts about mutant ants unleashed by a supervillain upon the presidential picnic on the White House lawn. (And let's face it, who wouldn't be taken by that concept?)

So if you are not careful, you'll end up on the wrong side of history on this one. That's why it's so hard to get a no. *Not right now,* yes; *Not my type of script,* sure; *I have another script like this,* why not? *It's great, but not for me,* all the time; but rarely a flat "no".

PAYING FOR FEEDBACK

People you pay will always have comments. Very few can take the time to read something and then just say, *"Perfect!"* I'm sure someone looked at the finished draft of *Citizen Kane* and said, *"Why does so much of it take place at the dining room table? Can you move it around a little, Orson?"*

And people who pay want validation, but also want their money's worth. If you don't find anything wrong, why did I pay you? So consultants, or readers, will look to find everything they can. If they find very little, then you've either done a fantastic job or they've done a terrible one.

Getting another pair of eyes can help, if the person's reputation and qualifications are good.

THE APPEARANCE OF HELP

You'll also find people who don't so much want to help as they want to *appear* to help. It may be with the best intentions, but time gets away from all of us.

If push comes to shove, they will, but usually your project just sits, unread, unwatched, uncriticized. Everyone has to look out for themselves.

> *I know so-and-so, let me pass your project along to him.*
> "Oh, great! You're sure it's no problem?"
> *No problem at all.*
> CUT TO: A couple of days later
> "Hey, have you passed that e-mail along yet?"
> *Well...*

As time goes on after making the promise to you, your friend has begun to worry about how he or she will be perceived. What if your script doesn't resonate with his contact as it has with him? How much does he know his contact? Does he want to use the connection for something like this?

Beware of the soft change of heart. *"I'm not sure if he's in town right now."* The connection begins to fade because you only want to use your connection for something you're sure about. Or, and I hate to admit that I've done it before, other things come up and you never get to what you promised as other things on your list take priority.

THANK YOU

Just like when you have a meeting or get a connection to give you their time, always thank your audience, whether it's a simple, verbal "thank you," or in a note. I've attended shows of (ex-)friends, and had them *not* thank me for paying money and taking my time to see their terrible shows.

Since there are so many people out there requesting your time, they need to do the extra things to appease their supporters, otherwise they'll have a hard time keeping their audience, especially when your show is not good in the first place.

CONCLUSION

It can't hurt to support others, mentally and physically. You'll feel inspired and get to see what's out there, not to mention what works and what doesn't. And you'll feel energized by others doing something. But you're no longer just an audience member.

You may be required to provide a service. Tread carefully. Remember, no one knows anything so who is anyone to say what's good or what's bad? Be diplomatic to your friends and when you need their thoughts, find someone whose opinion and judgement you trust and put your ego aside.

It's better to hear constructive criticism than just the usual *"You were great!"* even if it's small tweaks needed to improve or polish. Because "you were great!" doesn't help (unless there's no opportunity to tweak it, in which case it's recommended).

Both asker and askee must tango together. This is part of what makes LA so phony. The very nature of creativity and self-esteem depends on it.

Of course, if you ask a New Yorker, they'll tell you *"The stink coming off your performance made me think I was driving through Jersey"*. That's before they bought this book and learned the game, right?

CHAPTER 10 - MAINTAINING A SOCIAL LIFE

INTRO

Yes, your industry career can be a 24/7 grind, but that doesn't mean you can't build fun and relaxation into the equation. Sometimes, socializing takes the form of networking when you join some people you already know, with whom you can be more relaxed, but mostly it's just a brief respite from the day-to-day, a chance to enjoy yourself and do the things you like to do.

You're in luck! LA is one of the most abundant and diverse cities for that. There's soooo much to do that it is difficult to know where to begin.

WHAT'S YOUR PLEASURE?

In another city, one may have to spend six months indoors which leaves a *dearth* of choices, limited to either the local tavern or fitness club as a hangout perhaps. In LA, the environs are plentiful, the possibilities on how you can occupy your body and refresh your mind are endless. It's best to take advantage of the eternal sunshine and multitude of locales.

THE GREAT OUTDOORS

As we mentioned, Los Angeles is the most mountainous region in California. Thus you have ample opportunities to hike and/or camp outside the city, up the coast, overlooking the ocean, in the valleys, and even right in the middle of town. California has plenty of national forests (thank you, President Teddy "Rough Rider" Roosevelt).

Hiking

For the avid hiker, you have many options providing a selection of steep trails, long trails, picturesque vistas, historic landscapes, and whatever fits your hiking needs. Here are several sites where you can find trails that serve your hiking requirements best:

- www.discoverlosangeles.com

- www.modernhiker.com

- www.everytrail.com

- www.hikespeak.com

Camping

And for those who enjoy roughing it for a few days at a time, experiencing the sanctity of nature is within reach as there are plenty of popular campsites open to you.

You can start nearby with the three saints: Mount San Antonio (a.k.a. Mount Baldy) which contains the highest point in Los Angeles County, Mount San Gorgonio in San Bernadino County, and Mount San Jacinto in Riverside County. All three have great hiking and camping; Yosemite, Sequoia & Kings Canyon are great; and the famous Joshua Tree (where the streets have no name) is great for rock climbing and camping.

Death Valley is also a great place to camp, as long as you go there in the early spring.

And if you like mixing camping with swimming, surfing, windsurfing, surf fishing and beachcombing, check out Leo Carrillo in nearby Malibu.

Here is a List of Campsites for you to choose your own adventure: www.parks.ca.gov/.

CONCERTS

The best part of living in a big city like Los Angeles is that it's a must-stop destination for the biggest bands and musicians. If U2 or Madonna are touring, you can be sure they're gonna hit the Southland. The question is, which venue, and do you like it large or small?

Tucked inside the hustle and bustle of the densest part of the city, the Hollywood Bowl is one of the treasures of Los Angeles. If you're attending a concert there, you're lucky. Conversely, if you're trying to drive through Highland Avenue on the night of a concert, it can be your greatest enemy. (*Curse you, Summer Concert Series!*)

They have everything from sing-a-longs to the classical music from cartoons to all the big names on tour. The best fireworks show I've ever seen was at "the Bowl" one Fourth of July where Hall & Oates played a concert backed by the LA Philharmonic.

Similarly, there's the Greek Theatre in Griffith Park. But it doesn't stop there, as shows are held at Dodgers Stadium, the Home Depot Center in Carson, the Staples Center, and the newly repurposed Forum in Inglewood which now provides acoustically-perfect sound for the biggest of names.

Small Venues

And for the up-and-coming artists or the ones who are not as big as the big stadium bands, you have some wonderfully intimate music halls in which to experience them. The Mint, the Fonda, and any of those on the Sunset Strip among many others fall into this category. (Keep your eyes peeled in *LA Weekly* magazine for a calendar.)

My favorite part of this is, being that this is LA, you never know what surprise guests might appear alongside the featured act. One of my favorite moments came at the now-defunct Key Club on the Sunset Strip when The Presidents of the United States (*Lump, Peaches*) brought Weird Al Yankovic on stage to play a cover of Boston's *More than a Feeling*. He rocked the accordion while a fan blew his hair back with his trademark goofy flair. Priceless!

SPORTS

You already know that Los Angeles is flush with sports teams. Games represent wonderful opportunities for celeb sightings and they're always a fun time.

Try to find a friend who works for a company that has luxury box seats, or if you go to Dodgers Stadium, some of the biggest entertainment companies have tickets to seats that are actually *closer* to home plate than the pitcher's mound is.

NIGHTLIFE

What kind of big city would it be without nightlife? And a legendary nightlife it is to say the least, with stories of celebs partying until they're dead. Now, you certainly don't have to go *that* far; you can have a fun time and still wake up the next morning (or afternoon).

The Sunset Strip is a popular place to see the hip and trendy and to be seen. (That is, if you don't mind dark, loud, and crowded clubs.) Waiting in line to get in is a pain, but it's nothing compared to the line you wait in trying to get your car from the valet on a Friday or Saturday night when the clubs are closing down. The Strip becomes a parking lot.

By the way, don't be confused and think this is New York City where bars stay open so late that it's early. Bars in Los Angeles close at 2 because that is when California law cuts off alcohol sales, but last call is a good time earlier. The staff wants you out at 2. No sense in sticking around if they're not getting tips for serving.

If you are on the Sunset Strip at last call on a weekend, you'll probably be hanging around for a while, waiting for the valet to bring your car and then navigating traffic, so it will *feel* like last call is at 2.

If you absolutely must travel through West Hollywood one of these weekend nights, you should avoid Sunset like the plague.

Let's not ignore the relatively new DTLA destination -- LA Live. After all, they've put a lot of time and money into building it, so we might as well take advantage. It's "the most entertaining place on the planet" (according to their website).

And that barely scratches the surface. Many people head down to the South Bay for the younger, beach-going crowd and almost every neighborhood has local spots to frequent. Find your own happy place.

ENTERTAINMENT-RELATED PANELS

An LA exclusive! You can't get these elsewhere because this is where the stars live. On any given night, you can see a panel that includes the cast and creators of *Modern Family*, a famous comedian being interviewed by another famous comedian, the Emmy-nominated writers of television's top shows, a legend of Hollywood introducing his classic film on the anniversary of its release, or any random combination of famous guests speaking on a variety of topics.

Or get in good with a member of the Producer's Guild and you may get to attend a screening of a movie where the director or cast members are interviewed afterwards.

To stay up on the latest event news, you can subscribe to LA Talks," or "PaleyFest," or check out the WGA Foundation's webpage to fill your evenings.

FITNESS ORIGINALS

Is working out your escape/stress relief/solace? You can do things here that you can't do anywhere else. Rollerblade along the strand, practice yoga on the beach, or unleash your inner gymnast on the rings and parallel bars along Santa Monica's pier.

There's also The Stairs, a Santa Monica institution, aptly named because they are, quite simply, a set of stairs. (Actually, there are two sets.) They go from one street down below to another street. One set is concrete, the other is wood, and they contain approximately 200 steps. At any given time, you will see anyone from kids to professional athletes go up and down like zombies, mindlessly chugging along one step at a time.

Trainers bring their SUVs filled with workout equipment and open the trunk to incorporate everything else into running up and down those stairs. It's become quite the cottage industry.

This is where the "trainers to the stars" reside and you'll find all your famous fitness coaches here, plus any fitness class you've ever heard of such acroyoga, soulcycle, piloxing, and every other fad that's currently sweeping the nation.

Needless to say, there's also the one-and-only Muscle Beach, available to anyone who feels comfortable working out in skimpy leotards among chiseled physiques while tourists snap pictures of them. Feel free to purchase a pass to use the only outdoor weight room around.

And if that's not intense enough for you, there is a Crossfit "box" right next to where you live. (I'm confident in saying that because it seems there's a new one popping up daily in *every* neighborhood).

Not athletic? There's even a Crossfit for nerds (their selling point, not mine) in North Hollywood, for those who want more endurance than just watching a *Star Trek* marathon.

AND MORE

And that's not all! Pub trivia is huge, karaoke bars are abundant (especially in Koreatown where you can have your own room!), companies run scavenger hunts throughout the city and, of course, there's the popular Groupon, Living Social, and Amazon Local sites where you can literally find ANYTHING ELSE. If it's happening, you'll know about it.

MAKING PLANS

It may be difficult to find people to join you for events regularly, which is why a large network is better. Part of the problem is the geographic proximity and the other part is scheduling. Because of this, a relationship, even a solid friendship may only allow for seeing each other every six months if you don't run in similar circles or live in the same part of town.

LA is not a 9 to 5 town where everyone has their nights free. Industry players are always taking classes, going to shows, networking, and, *still* working later than they'd like. Matching a night off among you and your friends can be tricky.

If you're lucky, you'll have a friend that you can always count on for concerts, sporting events, or some other mutual passion. Even then, there is always stuff that comes up at the last second. So let's discuss this mentality, something to which I've alluded already.

FLAKING

For a while, planking was very popular, then it was photobombing, but the one thing that never goes out of style in Los Angeles is "flaking". It's here to stay. In fact, the stigma that the residents have here is that they are "flakey".

People say things like,

I'll be there!
Count me in.
See you then!

I remember the first time I realized these phrases were not to be taken literally. I stayed late at the office one evening because I would be heading right over to the comedy club to perform a set. One other assistant was still there working late before going to watch me perform. As I passed his desk on my way out, he said, "I'm right behind you".

The walk to my car was three minutes, the drive was seven minutes, and I was in the club within fifteen. He never showed. What happened in that fifteen minutes to keep him from fulfilling what was such a small promise that it doesn't even deserve mention is beyond me, but this is how quickly and easily people flake in LA.

People in Los Angeles want you to know that they *would* do something with you. They don't necessarily want to *actually* do anything with you. They'll talk about making plans, talk about planning to make plans, they may even *make* plans, but following through on those plans is where the train derails.

Even the nicest people you'll meet can fall into this behavioral pattern and then apologize profusely. (This is when they *actually* communicate their change of plans.) *I am soooooooooo sorry . . . Something came up that I can't get out of. . . Trust me, I would rather go to your thing.*

It is difficult living in a town with so many options and the possibility that every night, every moment, no matter how slight, holds a chance to further your career. Or it may be that something really cool came up. (Remember all that nightlife Los Angeles has to offer?) There still needs to be the integrity of committing to something and following through.

For those of you from out of town, it can be quite a shock. Where you come from, when someone says they're coming, they show up. If they do not, one of two things has happened: they have either been in a horrific accident making them unable to get word to you or they have screwed up and are terribly sorry. (Hey, it happens.)

When you are first flaked on by someone you genuinely like, it's disappointing. You say to yourself, *I like this person, but they must now be placed on the mental list of people you cannot count on.* You'll first question their motives and then question your own sanity for remaining friendly with them, especially when they do it again. Don't worry, it won't be as jarring as you spend more time here.

KNOW THIS: Get friends to pay up front.

An extra ticket to Steve Martin interviewing Martin Short on stage became available in my group. I asked my friend Phil who really REALLY wanted to go, but had made dinner plans with a friend of his. So he asked that I give him five minutes while he blew off this dinner.

Minutes later, he told me he got out of it. Though conflicted that he'd lost one friend, he was excited to join me . . . until he realized the event was at a theatre across town (the Alex) and not the one next door to him (the Aero), and so he then blew me off presumably to *un*flake on his now ex-friend. See, no big thang.

A rule I usually adhere to is "Yes" means "Maybe," "Maybe" means "No," and "No" means "No."

These examples, by the way, are not isolated, but everything in this book comes from repeated occurrences and validation from others who have experienced the same. Nor would I contend these examples are exclusive only to Los Angeles, but they are more the norm here. It's only one aspect of dating that makes it so difficult in Los Angeles.

DATING

Many people will tell you that dating in LA sucks, but the truth is, dating in LA sucks.

If you have a decent day job, you'll have your nights and weekends to date, but even then, script readers, agents, assistants, etc. may put you in second position behind a stack of scripts to read and people to meet after work or talent to scout. Their "free time" is spent trying to get ahead or stay afloat.

Then there's a very important aspect of dating, a term you'll hear often.

Geographically Undesirable

Remember that scene in *Swingers*? The guys discuss how someone's zip code indicates if they are someone you would want to date. In the dating game, the term "geographically undesirable" comes up a LOT. You may meet the perfect person, but if he or she is more than 5, or 10, or 20 miles (you will set your own parameters), then it's a non-starter.

Think about it – you can see each other evenings after work (assuming your schedules don't fluctuate too much), but if you take traffic into consideration, it makes it far more difficult. You leave work at 6 or 7, then you have to travel through rush hour traffic, arriving at 8 p.m. in time for a late dinner, and then have to hop back in your car to get enough sleep for the next day. It's a schlep.

Dating Up

There's an unrealistic expectation of dating in Los Angeles that you can find the perfect person, that every one of your criteria can be met. A friend relayed the all-too-familiar tale of the guy who was on a great date with this woman when she said, "This is the greatest date I've ever been on. I really like you. I only wish I could continue seeing you, but I only date men who are taller than me."

Was she saying this to be nice, or was this a genuine concern of hers? (Keep in mind, the height discrepancy was not extreme.) In other towns and all over the world, it's understood that you'll find a partner with qualities you like and some notasmuch. But here, in a city where most days are perfect, people are always looking to "date up". That is, whoever they have, they can find better. The next Chris Hemsworth and Beyoncé are out there somewhere, right?

The Business of Sexual Relations

This actually happens. I know, shocking, right? There are people who choose to supplement their talents with what some might categorize as "leaving nothing to chance". And there are people who are willing to allow that. (I'm talking about sleeping around in order to advance your career.)

If you're okay with it, you can certainly do it. There are some very famous and successful people who used this method to accelerate their careers. It is a nice steroid for talent and persistence. Just be wary that there are those who take advantage of people who opt for this method. But who am I, your dad? It's your life. Do whatever you want.

CONCLUSION

Allow yourself some "me time". Keeping your sanity requires down time, and LA provides more activities for this than any other town. When you plan to enjoy yourself, be wary of that time-honored LA tradition known as flaking.

Finding someone whose personality meshes with yours, has a complementary schedule *and* lives a reasonable distance from you can be your greatest accomplishment in town, even more than becoming famous. Just go with it.

CHAPTER 11 - TRANSPORTATION IN LA

INTRO

This section is longer than the others because of the disproportionate amount of time you'll spend in your car. LA's sprawled out unlike any other major city in the world. You have to get around somehow, so everyone encases themselves inside a four-wheeled box of chrome. Day after day, your car becomes an isolated paradise floating down the Rivers of Hades, each car only holding one person, such is our driving culture.

YOUR LIFEBLOOD

People frequently ask, *"Do you need a car in Los Angeles?"* And I tell them, "You need a car in Los Angeles."

And then they'll say, *"I talked to a guy who gets by without a car in Los Angeles."* And I'll say, "You NEED a car in Los Angeles."

"But," they'll say, *"I lived in New York and took the bus everywhere."* To that, I'll say, "YOU NEED A CAR IN LOS ANGELES!"

Any further conversation will get your nose tweaked and your butt wedgied. Stop being difficult!

There are certainly people without cars. And there are surgeons in Africa without sterilizing equipment. The cost and environmental reasons for living without wheels are quite clear, but why make it more difficult than you have to? Oh, sure, if you'd like to rely on Uber for everything, but busses may not show up when you expect them to and don't always travel routes that go where you need them to.

If you are determined, then yes, you can spend any money you have on Uber or transfer several times to get exactly where you need to go. How much time do you have? And waiting for the transportation to arrive, transferring, then waiting for *that* transportation to arrive, and walking the final distance to your destination, could take hours. Consider if a car trip takes 30 minutes, a bus will take at least 40 due to the regular stops.

So again, YOU NEED A CAR IN LOS ANGELES!!! Even if you only split it part-time with a friend. Otherwise, you are going to be either locked into a few areas or inconvenienced.

Now that you're on board with that, pay attention. Of course, the fact you NEED A CAR IN LOS ANGELES contributes to the fact it's the No. 1 city in terms of traffic.

Cars are more than just transportation items, they are also status symbols. *What* you drive somehow matters. A friend of mine who is a development executive for a literary manager would drive his brand new Volkswagen to lunch meetings, but park across the street instead of with the valet in front so his colleagues who drove luxury cars like BMWs, Mercedes, Lexuses (would it be Lexi? Lexim? Meh, whatever) would not see his car. It comes down to style over substance and keeping up your image.

Oh, and you need car insurance, too. LA's zip codes (which begin nine-double oh) represent the highest rates in the country so build that into your budget.

SWITCHING YOUR REGISTRATION

One of the first questions you'll have regarding your car is when you need to change over your registration to get your California plates. It's a big step, stripping you of your past and basically solidifying your status as a California resident (and paying more in insurance costs in the process).

As you drive around town, you will see A LOT of cars with out-of-state plates. Let's just say that these people are not all visitors. For whatever the reason – costs, nostalgia, pride – people will try to hang onto their old plates for as long as possible.

I'm not going to tell you what to do here because the DMV has their own ideas, but I did not switch my insurance or registration for about 16 months (which is when a driver without insurance ran a red light and smashed head first into me, totaling my car and forcing me to switch over my registration).

GETTING AROUND TOWN

Los Angeles has THE worst drivers in the country. This SHOULD NOT be debated. Every now and again, you'll get some native debate this fact. This is simply their pride speaking, but they're wrong. Don't even bother getting into an argument. Make no mistake, the drivers here are, hands down, *the worst*.

Some cities have "bad" drivers – Miami drivers drive irresponsibly fast and frequently with their blinkers on, Boston and New York drivers keep one hand on the wheel while the other is out of the window with middle finger extended – but LA has THE WORST.

There's no logic behind some of the things you'll see, things that you've never seen anywhere else, things that you'd think were perhaps part of some elaborate film shoot that you happened upon, like a director has given the stunt driver their instructions:

> *"Okay, we're gonna need you to make a left turn across four lanes of traffic then stop short and swerve back across four lanes onto the off ramp, before you realize that's not your exit and you hop the median to get back into traffic. We'll cue the extras in their cars but let it get so busy before you start, forcing them to either slam on their brakes or jackknife into you at 40 miles an hour. You ready? And . . . ACTION!!!"*

I'm not saying it's the natives who cause this. There are people from all over, many from nations or cities that have different rules or that don't have a driving culture (or cars for that matter). But there's also that entitlement we spoke of where people feel they can do whatever they want and that carries over to driving.

Perhaps this is because when you spend so much time in a car, the last thing you want to do is spend more time there, so you break the rules in order to get somewhere faster. *Or* maybe the sun has just baked everyone's brain. (It's probably a deadly combination of both.) I would never be surprised if I were to see someone run a red light, plow into a pedestrian, and then yell at the pedestrian for damaging their car.

My favorite thing to see is someone in an Italian sports car (with the ability to go from 0 to 200 if you even *think* of taking your foot off the brake) crawling along the city streets in bumper-to-bumper traffic. That's like buying an airplane and driving it everywhere. See, people gotta *look* good no matter how impractical.

Now, understanding that, let's start with the basics. Some rules may be different from your hometown, and you should know these.

A Grid

LA is basically laid out in a grid, with a few areas that deviate from that just to confuse you (Silverlake, I'm looking at you!) where, like Greenwich Village in New York City, it gets wonky in places which can completely throw you off. And there are other quirks such as Santa Monica which is North of Wilshire . . . until it is South of Wilshire. It's like the Broadway of LA (east of 7th Avenue until it's west).

The Left Turn

You'll see things you have never seen before in Los Angeles. For instance, most cities have a dedicated left hand turn arrow at intersections. You're instructed to stay behind the line until it's your time to turn. Out here, you pull forward *into* the intersection and wait for oncoming traffic to subside before making your turn. This is *after* those cars have stopped and before the cross traffic starts. Fun, right? (Oh, and now your light has turned red so you'd better turn already!)

The first thing a friend told me is to make a game of it. "Your job is to pull as many cars as you can," he said. That means, the instant that oncoming traffic has stopped, you make your turn and maybe two, maybe *three* cars will follow. Several times, you'll look in the rearview mirror and see a fourth car behind you, usually about to get jack knifed by oncoming cars since they ran the red very blatantly in an effort to save 30 seconds of their day.

Of course, this practice remains dangerous for several reasons. One is the fact drivers continue to stream through the light as it turns yellow and then red (for spending another cycle at that intersection can send any driver over the edge), leaving you stuck in the intersection as cross traffic now begins to move towards you, because they sure as hell aren't going to spend any more time waiting.

To add an obstacle, every so often some cockeyed driver with no equilibrium or depth perception will lean to the left, preparing for the turn, so far left, in fact, that it he is *in* the oncoming traffic lane. Now you have to enter the lane to your right in an effort to avoid them and the head on collision they're about to cause.

The whole dance requires cross traffic to wait a full three beats after your light has turned green to be sure the intersection is clear of Kamikaze drivers before proceeding. (This may be due to caution or just looking at smart phones.) If, after a count of "three Mississippi," the lead car has not gone, you are welcome to honk. (Or sooner if you're from the Northeast and you are used to honking the instant the light changes.)

Right on Red

You can take a right on red here, *if* there is not a sign declaring otherwise. Go ahead. It's legal. This is probably the greatest feeling in the world for New Yorkers. Please stop first and look BOTH ways, making sure the coast is clear before proceeding. You laugh, but this is not a common practice so it cannot be stated enough. Drivers look left as they turn right and forget that there are other people on the planet, more specifically, in the cross walk directly in front of them.

Blinkers

By observing the typical flow of traffic, you would think that blinkers are not standard issue on cars out here. I had been here less than a week when I was driving a friend who grew up here. He saw me put on my blinker and asked why I had done that. "Why did I put on my blinker? Uh, because I'm making a turn." He laughed and explained they didn't do that here. They're basically thumbing their collective noses at that oppressive auto-safety industry.

The "California Stop"

Forget blinkers, so many drivers don't recognize the red and white octagonal signs positioned at the ends of the blocks that it's been given a name – the "California stop". This is where you slow down, and maybe think about stopping, but never really cease forward movement. *I'm already way over the line so why not just keep going?* It's as if they saw a bed of nails ahead of them, but quickly realized it's only a paper bag. So their precious car will not have to employ its brake pads they think will disintegrate upon use.

Traffic Cameras

Many intersections used to be equipped with traffic cameras in case you thought that a red light was merely a suggestion (which many people do). They are taking most of them down, mainly because the actors in town running red lights for a free head shot thought the photo didn't "accurately portray my sense of whimsy".

That is in the City of Los Angeles. Independent cities not bound by the rules of Los Angeles may still use them. So be wary. If you come upon an intersection with one and are over the line, into the intersection after the light has turned red, a flash will go off, then another (Smile! You're on camera.), and you will receive an exorbitant fine in the mail which you will then contest.

Going "Over the Hill"

There will come a time when you will need to get "over the hill". That means you must visit the valley or return from the valley. From Los Angeles, there are essentially six direct ways to do that — the 101, the 405, Sepulveda Boulevard, Laurel Canyon (which stems from Crescent Heights north of Sunset), Coldwater Canyon (which stems from Beverly Drive also at Sunset), and Beverly Glen (which remains Beverly Glen throughout, go figure).

You will find out which works for you in terms of geography and time of day, and also which one you like best. Do you like to feel like a NASCAR driver, twisting and turning, slowing and speeding up around each curve? Then, by all means, take one of the surface streets.

Or do you just like a straight shot, regardless of traffic? If so, the freeways are for you. Stop and go, stop and go. (If you get it at a decent time, then the freeway is a no-brainer.)

If it's raining, the fun of swerving up and down the hills and taking your life in your hands is turned up a notch.

Construction

The city is always under construction. And that's without lane closures for productions (though this doesn't get in the way as much as you might think).

Gas Prices

They are always among the highest in the country. Supply and demand.

Motorcycles

Motorcyclists are allowed to weave in and out of lanes making traffic less of a problem for them and getting knocked off their bikes more of one. (I've actually never seen this happen, but given that they sneak up on you while you're in bumper-to-bumper traffic lamenting all previous life decisions, it's a wonder it doesn't happen more often.)

Electric Vehicles

LA is a leader in electric vehicles. Teslas are springing up everywhere. More and more garages and parking lots provide electric charging stations. Take advantage . . . PLEASE!

Compact Car Parking Spaces

Taking a rough estimation, I would say there are about 5 million compact car spaces throughout town, but only about 500,000 compact cars on the road. It's fun to see the huge cars cram into these spaces like Chris Farley in *Tommy Boy*. ("Fat guy in a little coat.")

20 Minutes

Every place in and around Los Angeles is 20 minutes away. When somebody asks you how far away something is, the answer is always "20 minutes". This is not an exaggeration.

- Pasadena to Burbank? 20 minutes.
- Hollywood to Culver City? 20 minutes.
- Pasadena to Hollywood? 20 minutes.
- Santa Monica to Beverly Hills? 20 minutes.
- Santa Monica to Manhattan Beach? 20 minutes.
- Venice to Sherman Oaks? 20 minutes.

See the pattern? Okay, most of those take longer than that. It's just an easy answer which has the *potential* to be accurate. The thing to remember here is that these estimates do not account for traffic. There are few things guaranteed in this world and LA traffic is one of them (death and taxes being the others). And then, on top of the typical traffic, there's rush hour traffic. Typical traffic can add 15 minutes and, for rush hour traffic, you'll want to add 15 and then double that total.

So if it takes you 20 minutes to go from Santa Monica to Glendale on a Sunday morning, you can imagine it will take an hour and twenty minutes to do so during rush hour. (I apologize for the math.)

Rush Hour

It used to be that rush hour would get going after 5, maybe as early as 4, but now streets start to back up as early as 2. Then, on Fridays, all bets are off. People can't get out of work fast enough, especially at the beginning of a holiday weekend.

Weekends will find a lot of traffic as well. If you are going anywhere, try to go there before 10 a.m. After that, the city's a zoo. (Ironically enough, the City Zoo, is not too busy.) You'll have a couple more hours on Sundays while people do brunch, Farmer's Markets, and/or church.

This knowledge is especially important if you are trying to hightail it out of town for a brief respite from the LA craziness, whether to Vegas or San Diego.

Crosswalks

You need to stop for pedestrians in a crosswalk. That said, as a pedestrian, do *not* assume that anyone will stop. Only step into a lane when you are sure that traffic in that lane has stopped. See that the driver is looking at you. (Check two or three cars deep per lane to make sure they have stopped because drivers lose track of crosswalks while checking their Facebook pages and may slam into the stopped car in front of them causing that car to hit you.) Officially, cars should not proceed until the entire crosswalk (both sides) is clear.

As an intelligent pedestrian, you should watch out for Numero Uno. Of course, this is LA, and intelligent pedestrians are a novelty.

Many LA drivers are actually quite respectful of pedestrians on crosswalks. Those are not the ones who you will remember.

Jaywalkers

The first time you see people standing on the curb with no cars in sight waiting for the light to change is a curious moment. Then, you become conditioned and don't think anything of it. You become the person standing there waiting for the light to change. You are not to step off the curb, even if you are in a crosswalk, until the walk sign is on. There are still plenty of jaywalkers, as there are everywhere, but here, you can get a ticket.

Officially, it's illegal, but so is counting cards in Vegas. (Players gonna try to beat the system.) Also considered illegal jaywalking is entering a crosswalk *after* the "Don't Walk" sign has begun blinking. It's not often that you will get busted for that, but be wary of this inane rule. Traffic cops downtown are notorious for "mugging" you. A recent article in the *LA Times* said as much.

If you do get a traffic ticket, by the way, and wish to contest it, always choose to do so in writing. If you go to court to fight it, the judge will side with the cop 90% of the time regardless of how egregiously the cop misrepresents the facts.

When you consider the illogical driving maneuvers you see daily, jaywalking makes no sense. At least if you're in a car and someone does something crazy and illegal, you'll have some metal protecting you. When you're jaywalking, it's just skin and bones (assuming you are not a cyborg). Why risk your life to cut down on a few seconds? It's too bad you can't run jaywalkers down as that would fix several problems and make the afternoon commute that much more fun.

Maybe it's all part of a reality show. Maybe these people are looking to be hit as creative inspiration in an effort to make the news, which they will then parlay into a sitcom deal. "HE's a non-thinking, brainless moron who stepped into rush hour traffic . . . SHE'S the no-nonsense surgeon who reattached his spleen. NOW they're odd couple roommates."

And as you keep one eye open for jaywalkers, your other eye (my apologies if you are a Cyclops) will witness a cornucopia of things that'll make you shake your head.

TEN WORST MANEUVERS

In almost two decade here, I am still stunned on a daily basis. It seems almost unfathomable, but drivers are becoming more incompetent. For a fairly well-functioning society, you'll see some idiotic stuff.

The Sudden U

As a biker, this one could not piss me off more. Technically a U-Turn is illegal, unless at an intersection that allows it. But hey, sometimes we smack our heads and say, *"Ooops, I needed to go the other way."*

It wouldn't be bad if it were done with a level of competence, but there's nothing sadder than seeing someone do this across FIVE lanes of traffic (two lanes in each direction plus a turn lane in the middle), thus pissing off five lanes of drivers. You have to be a special case of self-absorbed to be able to accomplish this.

Revisiting the fact that when you are "pulling" two cars behind you through the intersection it becomes even worse. The cars behind you are all speeding up to make it through the intersection in time before getting jackknifed by oncoming traffic. And here you are, slamming on your brakes in an effort to reverse direction. It goes against all the rules. Until cars are equipped with U-Turn signals, *don't do it*. (Even then, no one would signal anyway.)

Righthand Turn from the Lefthand Lane (and Vice Versa)

Whatever the make and model of a car, it's something you should not drive if you can't drive like a normal person. Cars have power steering now and making a right turn should be made from the right lane (unless you are commanding a big rig). Streets and cars have been designed for this. You don't need any added momentum, or even a physics degree. Yet you regularly see drivers move to the left before making a right turn.

Such thinking has caused me to believe that we need more restrictions on driver's licenses. Right now, it's for corrective lenses and large trailers. If you are driving a commercial vehicle, you need to pass another test. But cars have become so big and cumbersome (i.e. Escalades, Hummers, Suburbans, et al.) that they should have their own zip codes. Have you seen some of the people behind the wheel looking totally overwhelmed? They were given a license to drive a *car*, not a riverboat on wheels. They should be restricted to Mini Coopers or Fiats. It's simply a side effect of bad regulations.

Couple that with the cluelessness and entitlement of drivers here and the effects are maddening.

The Fade

As we know, blinkers are not used in Los Angeles. (I use mine, but I'm weird.) And it's bad enough to make a lane shift ahead of someone without warning them. Sometimes it's an accident, with the blind spot and all that, but many times, people just decide to switch lanes unannounced because it's *their* road, obviously. Other people just sort of fade into a new lane.

It's virtually imperceptible at first, since they move so slowly toward you. You may even notice, but have faith that they are going to correct themselves before it's too late. Notsomuch. Regardless of if they are about to hit you, they're just gonna keep fading.

The Self-Serving Left

On many of the main drags in Los Angeles, you have a stop light every second or third block. These stop lights make it easier for cars to take a left from the side street. And so why would you go one block down for an easy logical turn when you can inch out across three lanes of traffic and risk your life and piss off literally dozens of cars to do the same thing? Seems like a no-brainer to me. I mean to say these people *are* no-brainers.

The Blockade

Speaking of a lack of brains, the blockade features someone who should not be anywhere near a car, let alone behind the wheel of one.

As traffic flows mind-numbingly throughout the day, a driver may not consider, while remaining glued to the bumper in front of them, that they are now in an intersection as the light is about to change. Sometimes it's unavoidable as you may not have imagined the slow flow would prevent you from clearing the intersection in time, but it's what happens next that's inexcusable.

A car is bumper-to-bumper with the car in front of them, blocking oncoming traffic, BUT the lane next to them IS CLEAR. In fact, it has space enough for several cars! Oncoming traffic honks at the car urging it to move over a lane, but these people stare straight ahead, clueless to any logical solution, continuing to selfishly piss off all these other drivers. I've even seen people get out of their cars (there's time to do so with the idiots blocking all traffic) and point to the open lane.

What are these people afraid of? You move into the other lane and then you can immediately move back into your lane once traffic starts to move. It boggles the mind.

The Cut-and-Pray

There's a subset of self-serving lefters that shoot out into traffic when they get their chance, disregarding the fact that many drivers may not see them (for a variety of reasons — texting, a car low to the ground, the fact that you're *inexplicably darting into traffic*, common sense, etc.) and pray that all lanes stop for them. This is actually the main cause of heart attacks in town and drivers on the other side of the road who also crap themselves upon seeing the "stones" of these morons.

Game of Chicken

Hollywood contains many narrow streets that have enough room for a parked car on each side and two cars traveling in opposite directions . . . barely. (If one car is an SUV, it won't work.) It sets up a classic game of Chicken. Many drivers don't let this slow them down as they head directly at you. If you can, pull in front of a driveway or just slam on your brakes. It may not stop them from hitting you, but at least the whiplash won't be as bad.

Peek-a-Boo

You see the car. It's coming out of a side street, edging toward the main road. You're about a block and a half away. The car sits there patiently. *Does it even want to turn right?* you wonder as you continue along, closing at a normal speed. *If it does, why hasn't it done so already? It's had plenty of time.* And then, just as you are close enough to pick a leaf off its windshield, PEEK-A-BOO! That's when they cut out into the street causing you to either test your brakes or recreate a scene from the *Dukes of Hazard.*

The Dead Stop

Usually, this is used only when an emergency vehicle is around. Cars just stop. They do not pull over to allow the life-saving vehicles a path to get by. In fact, many times they look confused as to why the siren-flashing car is barreling toward them so brazenly. It's . . . not . . . hard! Get . . . over!

The worst thing anywhere is when someone does something illegal or idiotic like cutting you off, stopping traffic for blocks, and giving you the finger after you apply the horn. These people are owning the fact they're entitled assholes. I like to say they're doubling down on asshole. (Obviously, adding smartphones to the mix of incompetence has not helped matters.) But this is not restricted to the streets of the Southland.

ROAD RAGE

Being crammed behind the wheel so often contributes to the already short fuse you have. Seeing all the lunacy can get people hot real fast.

People will literally weave in and out of traffic in order to catch you and let you know how angry they are. Even if you were in the right, someone might consider you their arch nemesis for a day.

One important note: if you are ever bumped or involved in a fender bender, always get the other car's license plate *before* pulling over to the side of the road. This is due to the fact that there's a good chance the other driver will just take off as you're pulling over to do the legal and moral thing.

I like to focus on how the bad drivers can bring people together. If your windows are open, you can turn to the driver next to you, also stuck lamenting some driver's stupidity and bond with them over said stupidity. In the isolated world of driving in Los Angeles, it's a moment you can feel like a member of the commuting community as some would do on the train in, say, Washington DC or Chicago.

WHY ARE LA DRIVERS THE WORST?

This is a question that you'll ruminate on with friends from time to time. And there's no one *definitive* answer, but there are several theories one might consider.

Self-absorption

This goes along with the entitled feel. Everyone is into themselves too much to care about anyone around them, and that includes rules that have been created for a society to run smoother when everyone cooperates. There is no introspection at all which transcends driving and speaks to the industry as a whole.

There's an old joke you may have heard about the Hollywood executive who runs a red light, and clips another car causing his own Mercedes to slam into a telephone pole, totaling his vehicle. When the rescue staff arrive, the executive is ranting, "Look what that guy did to my car! Do you know how much that car cost me?!"

The EMT says, "Sir, you need to calm down! You've had your arm severed in the accident."

The executive looks at where his arm used to be and says, "FUCK! My Rolex!"

New Drivers

Many drivers have never been behind a wheel before and are now forced to do so since, as I've mentioned previously, you need a car in Los Angeles. Unfortunately, like stand-up comedy, LA is not a place to start using a car, mainly because of the bad drivers. You should refine your skills in Montana first, or some other state where the only thing you might hit is a fencepost.

Overmatched by the Vehicle

Status means everything while practicality means nothing. Therefore, too many people have cars that enhance their standing, regardless of the fact that they cannot handle them. The city has tried to leave subtle hints around town such as more compact car parking spaces, but people still want their enormous monstrosities on wheels. This is usually worse for the reasonable driver since the practical car that one can handle is easily demolished by the out-of-control SUV.

Smart Phones

This is the new normal everywhere and not just in Los Angeles. An added element of permanent distraction was definitely not what this town needed. You'll see so many people hold the phone in front of them as if this "hands free" way of talking were any better since their hands are clearly *not free.*

Navel Gazing

A common term that speaks to an entire industry based on beauty and insecurity. Hence, it's more important to keep one eye in the mirror and another looking for celebrities than it is both eyes on the road.

So now that you are completely paranoid, here's how you can spend less time on the road.

AVOIDING TRAFFIC (As well as one can)

Given that everyone is in their cars at the same time, traffic is inevitable. But that doesn't mean you can't alleviate the pain, even if only by a small amount.

One thing you should not do is wait for the city to do something about it. The large project to expand the 405 freeway (including the now legendary "carmageddon," the day the freeway was closed) is completed. "It will alleviate traffic forever!" they said, in spite of the experts who said that by the time the expansion was done, it would not be wide enough and therefore not alleviate anything. So . . . there's that.

And with the also soon-to-be-completed and operational Metro Expo Line (expected in 2016) stretching all the way to the Santa Monica beach and providing a much-needed alternative to cross-town car traffic, there are new condominium complexes being built left and right which, once those new residents decide the light rail doesn't work for them, will also clog the roads.

Who knows? It could alleviate traffic altog—ah, hahah! I'm just kidding. It'll never be good. And that will add to the circus that is driving in LA.

You need to be proactive and wily to avoid the heaviest roads. There are certain directions at certain times that go "against the traffic" which will give your commute a more reasonable feel. This is barring an accident, of course. (See: Worst Drivers in the Country.)

Going "against traffic," does help . . . a little. You will still spend WAY too much time in your car, but you'll get to laugh at the schmoes on the other side of the road pulling their hair out as you coast along closer to the speed limit.

For instance, going south on the 405 from the valley after work is easier than going north. (It only starts piling up near Wilshire Boulevard.) But going from the Westside toward Hollywood after work is bad. Really, anywhere in Hollywood is bad. You must aim outward. Going toward the center spells disaster. In that case, you might want to pack a snack with you, and maybe an empty bottle for those, er, bladder emergencies.

Expect traffic to get congested around a highway on-ramp. Any entrance represents the potential for a logjam, but if you're not taking the on-ramp, you may find clear sailing ahead if you can get as far from the exit lane as possible.

Some roads are better to take than others. Side streets, for example. They give the impression of avoiding traffic, because you are moving steadily, though you do hit a stop sign at every block. Eventually, you have to make it back onto a main road. Could it be that you'll join it *after* the heaviest traffic has dissipated?

Always check www.sigalert.com before leaving or add the Waze app to your smartphone to give you an idea how screwed you will be. With that in mind, you should be able to move more fluidly through the city during the heaviest traffic times. Though if it rains, all bets are off.

RAINY DAY TRAFFIC

You will literally hear newscasters say, "*Do not go out if you don't have to.*" It's rain, people, not a zombie apocalypse. (I think residents here would actually do better in a zombie apocalypse than a steady rain.)

If it rains, people tend to "protect" themselves from the rain by leaving more space than usual between themselves and the curb. Of course, that philosophy neglects to take into consideration the fact they are not alone on the road. Part of this is reasonable (remember the drainage issues?), but if you are on a street with multiple lanes, when you move further out, you invade the lane next to you and the car next to you has to, in turn, move further out. Eventually, one of the cars will be in oncoming traffic. But that's okay, because they're doing the same thing. Now they're in your lane at the same time that you're in their lane. Hence, if you're looking to avoid an accident, a rainy day is not your best bet.

It might make the most sense if Los Angeles adopted British driving laws on days when it rains. But that would only confuse matters. The idea is to try to get the basics of driving down first before becoming advanced.

PARKING ENFORCEMENT

When I mentioned this book to friends, the one comment I kept hearing was, *"You have to mention parking enforcement."* So you know this is something that concerns people.

To this point, you may have noticed that I've taken my shots at agents, and even alluded (read: stated outright) that they are the worst people in town. I was being hyperbolic. Most agents are doing the best they can and are, in fact, human, with a heart and everything. This is not the case with the Parking Enforcement Bureau.

Short of mob-style executions, they are as close to the mafia as you'll see in LA. They have a pretty good racket going, which includes extortion (the practice of obtaining something, especially money, through force or threats), and run unchecked.

Think I'm kidding? You'll find out real fast, either first hand, or from a conversation with someone that one of the biggest areas of frustration in Los Angeles is with Parking Enforcement. Mention them to anyone and the first thing you'll hear is a curse word (even if you're talking to nuns).

It's not so much the fact that there are rules you must adhere to, but rather it is that they are actively trying to catch you breaking the rules by any means necessary.

Their tricks include using meters that do not allow you to refeed them; meters that reset when a car leaves and do not allow the next car any of the remaining time; chalking your tires at their discretion without any oversight; and I've seen tickets given out *before* meters have expired.

Dealing with parking rules and regulations will occupy more time than you deserve to spend, from trying to read and understand the signs to contesting the tickets, looking for parking that is legal, and paying the tickets. I'm sure they have some inherently decent henchmen simply doing their jobs but, from top to bottom, it's a racket.

KNOW THIS: Watch your back, Jack!

There was even a case where a judge ruled against the City of Los Angeles for farming out the processing of their appeals. You read that correctly – their appeals process is *against the law*. Legally, you have a case to fight them. But you cannot do it because they ignore the courts. (Still think it's a legitimate organization?)

Santa Monica and West Hollywood are the worst because they are their own cities. Culver City took one sign down because it was so confusing, but is equally evil. Beverly Hills doesn't even post their rules on the streets. You need to know that after 2 a.m., if you don't get a parking pass from a resident, you're screwed.

At one point, you will be unjustly given a ticket. Another time, you will lament the confusing signs that you THOUGHT you understood. Then, you will kick yourself for not remembering what the confusing sign meant and parking there anyway. Even if you manage to comprehend the rules of that specific area, you may feed the meter until 3. Go back at 2:45. Surprise! You've got a ticket.

The foot soldiers have their quota to reach. To that end, there are some streets where two cars are circling at the same time. I've even seen parking officers in a stare-down with drivers parked on a secluded side street two minutes before it would be legal, ready to ticket them if the drivers walked more than five feet from their cars. It is insidious.

Five Helpful Hints to Avoiding a Ticket

This constant swarm of glorified hall monitors coupled with confusing and contradictory signage that includes inconsistent parking rules that vary from street to street and town to town make avoiding a ticket more difficult than making it in Hollywood.

Here are some tips on how to avoid being put in a bad mood immediately:

1. Read the signs (paying special attention to a.m. & p.m.). Don't skim!
2. Overpay the meter.
3. Set the timer on your phone and arrive back early.
4. When parking on a hill, turn the wheels to the curb.
5. Watch out for street cleaning days. (If there are an inordinate number of available spaces on one side of the street, chances are, it's a street cleaning day.)

There are days when your brain is going in a million different directions and sometimes you just get burned by one of these things. Don't sweat it. I work two to three tickets into my budget every year. Such is life in LA.

PUBLIC TRANSPORTATION

Believe it or not, there is an extensive public transit system in Los Angeles, and it's expanding. LA is now in a concerted effort of doing what they actually had undone some 60 years ago when they allowed Detroit automakers to convince them to become a car culture. This seemed smart at the time as Los Angeles was not the urban landscape populated (polluted?) by outsiders as it is now. It may not always be convenient, depending on the distance you'll have to travel, but it is a fairly reliable alternative to the single-occupancy vehicle method.

Your public transit options can be broken down three ways:

- Bus/light rail (i.e. subway)
- Commuter rail
- Regional bus lines

Utilizing all three of these should bring you anywhere you'd like to go in the county and beyond . . . eventually. The problem is that it can take twice as long or greater than it would in your car. The cost-reward doesn't always add up.

In *general*, if you are going downtown, then it behooves you to take public transit to save on parking fees and traffic headaches. But you also have to live on a public transit line. Otherwise, you have to park somewhere, then hop on the line, then go downtown . . . Meh. You might as well just drive down there.

Even when the light-rail to the ocean is complete, there are wide patches of the city which will remain unconnected. This is not like Boston or New York where the subway lines have branches that can get anywhere without walking too far. The worst case scenario is you have to park your car at some outlet lot (or bike) to be connected.

And LA is such a sprawling city that there may not be a direct line to anyplace of import to you. For instance, if you live in a place like Santa Monica, you will still have to take the light rail an hour east (to downtown) and transfer in order to then go an hour south to get to LAX or Long Beach.

So let's take a closer look at your options for when you just want to leave the car at home and let the city drive you.

METRO

This is the city's main bus line and light rail provider. The busses run frequently, but it could take a couple of transfers on any given day, unless you just need to go straight down one of the main boulevards like Ventura or Santa Monica. And keep in mind, 40 minutes of riding on the bus may take a total travel time of 2 hours as you wait for each leg of the transfer. But, in theory, this can ease your burden and relax your mind in the day-to-day world of LA traffic.

As for the light-rail system, it's still fairly new as far as rail-based systems across the country go. The good news is that it's soooo clean. (It is not as contaminated by passengers as are subway cars in other major cities.)

The system is expanding and you will soon find it running through the Miracle Mile, into Culver City, and bringing you all the way to Santa Monica where that city is preparing by turning Santa Monica Place into a destination mall for dining and entertainment to compete with neighboring Third Street Promenade which is filled with entertainment and dining.

For all METRO related information, go to www.metro.net.

Metrolink

Not to be confused with METRO, this is the commuter rail system. If you spend your entire time in and around Los Angeles proper, you'll never know this exists. It is utilized mainly by people who commute to work from the outer perimeter of LA County (and into any of the neighboring counties).

Make sure you check the up-to-date transfer rules between the two companies because they change regularly and it can get confusing going between Metro and any of the regional lines.

There are many who believe this option is overpriced and constantly alienating clients by raising rates, but if you find yourself in places with names like San Bernadino, Moorpark, Palmdale, or Ontario, you should look into this option.

For information about Metrolink, go to www.metrolinktrains.com.

Regional Bus Lines

METRO does not go everywhere, but it will connect you with other bus services. Depending on where you live or work, you may need to use one of these many local providers for public transportation.

There is a preconceived notion that public transit such as the busses are only for dirty, poor people, and yes, while you will, at times, catch a whiff of something so putrid it can wipe your memory clean or witness someone yelling at his pet ferret that isn't really there, the service is safe, it's inexpensive, and gives you a much-needed break from behind the wheel. I'd recommend trying it every so often.

BIKING

What better place to bike than a city that never rains! There are a few top-notch biking communities – Long Beach, Pasadena, Santa Monica, the beach cities – and why shouldn't there be? You can bike through the streets and get your daily dose of Vitamin D at the same time.

You'd be surprised how a bicycle can cut down on commute times. Naturally, this depends on where you live and how far you are going. Say you want to go to Third Street Promenade in Santa Monica. Traffic going into all the parking garages begins to back up on Lincoln (i.e. five blocks away). Many cars are stuck at a light for two or more cycles and then take another ten minutes inside the parking garage before they can pull into a parking space. Factor in another few minutes to walk down six flights of stairs and over to whichever store you want to go.

If you take a bike, you can just cut through all that traffic and park in front of the store. Easy.

For required accessories, helmets are not required over 18, but a front head light is after dark. Tail lights are not required, but are recommended. The complete rules for biking can be found at www.bicyclela.org. There is also a helpful map of bike lanes there.

Yes, bicycling is big in the Los Angeles area and becoming bigger. And with that, bicycle thievery is also a big industry. Lock your bike! Choose a U-lock and not one of those thin "dental floss-type" locks. Be sure to secure your wheel with your frame. (Crooks like to take wheels, too.)

Bikes are stolen all the time. Even if you park it in your building's bike room or bike locker, if it's not chained up to something that cannot be moved, it WILL get stolen. Get a bike license in order to track your bike, though even if you do, the police will not be able to recover your bike should it get stolen. It's still inexpensive and could benefit you.

If you do have a front light and tail light, it's best to remove these when you leave the bike because, as easy as it is to steal bikes, it's even easier to steal lights from it. You might wonder who wants a stupid bike light. Everyone, apparently.

Purchasing a bike can be a good investment as more and more bike lanes are popping up everywhere. You can even take your bicycle on public transport in order to combine alternative forms of transportation on your trip. It is good exercise and saves money on gas which is a big savings.

Bike Lanes

There are three kinds of bike lanes: dedicated bike paths, dedicated bike lanes, and share the road lanes. Now, streets with "sharrows" are popping up everywhere too. This means a bike or a car can drive in a full lane.

Even though the bike path along the beach allows no cars on it, you still must be extra careful. It's a winding path and everyone is going at a different pace, from tandem bikes to kids just learning to ride on training wheels, to professional cyclists, to rollerbladers, joggers, and walkers. Add to that tourists and their children who have no idea what's going on meandering across the path like it's a mall concourse.

There is a saying that goes, "There are two types of bikers – those that have been hit by a car, and those that will be."

Drivers v. Bikers

Many people who bike think it gives them carte blanche to make up their own rules, which creates conflict with drivers, many of whom are ignoring driving laws at the same time. (Still the worst drivers in the country. Nothing's changed since earlier in the chapter.)

There are true bikers out there, bikers who know the code, the rules, and ride defensively; then there are those people who merely *own* a bicycle and use it sometimes. The latter are the ones who weave in and out of lanes, and blow through stop signs as if they weren't there. If you bike, you should know the FIRST law is that you are NOT a pedestrian. Bikers need to ride WITH traffic, not against it as runners are supposed to do.

It simply amazes me that bikers would not even think about stopping at a stop sign or intersection, even with cross-traffic. Given that many motorists don't pay heed to stop signs either, I keep expecting these bikers to get splattered. Every now and again, a cop will cite a biker for going through a stop sign or red light.

Many drivers will pause for you to go, but there are drivers (hopefully few and far between) who are just looking for an excuse to run down a biker. Or mainly, drivers are clueless and have no idea bikers exist.

There is a rule in place requiring a driver to leave a minimum of three feet when passing a bicyclist, but if they don't know bikers exist, it's safe to say they don't know about the three-foot rule.

The moral of the story is know the bike rules and bike with caution. There's reason to be worried, but if you know the rules and remain alert, you will be fine.

WALKING

I'm not sure I understand what you mean here. What is this "walking" you speak of? There's a song by the group Missing Persons called *Nobody Walks in LA*. That is accurate. Even if it makes more sense to walk (and it frequently does), it is simply not done.

If I do not have my bicycle handy, my philosophy is I will walk up to one mile, maybe even a mile and a half. This seems reasonable to me. (But what do you expect? I'm a nutbag, apparently.)

CONCLUSION

Los Angeles is very accessible via a variety of transportation options, most of which you will ignore in favor of your car that you MUST HAVE! (Okay, so it's *possible* to get by without a car if you have a steady job that lies on a transit line near apartment or you work from home, but it will not be that convenient.) Once inside your car, you will curse everything about the process of getting somewhere, from the traffic to the comically bad and selfish drivers to the corrupt Parking Enforcement Bureau.

Every day is a battle between other drivers, jaywalkers, and bicyclists. It's enough to make you want to stay at home in your pajamas . . . but you don't because that would be silly.

Maintain a laissez faire attitude. It's not worth it. At the same time, when you're on the front lines, keep your head on a swivel, and make sure your insurance is paid up.

CHAPTER 12 - CELEB SIGHTINGS

INTRO

Hollywood is home to many celebrities. Yes, seeing them loses its luster eventually since they're everywhere, but it's always good for a Facebook post to your friends back home, so be on the lookout and keep a list because they'll want to know. Heck, even those of us who've been here a while are always interested in a celeb sighting. It constitutes a decent percentage of our conversations. *"I saw so and so at the Beverly Center the other day. Seemed like a cool guy."*

It happens more often than you're aware. Celebs may be dressed down and you don't recognize them or you don't know who they are, or maybe they're less important than they think they are and you haven't missed anything.

Depending on your frequent hangouts and routines, you can see anyone from bit players (*"Hey, aren't you that guy from that thing?"*) to top dogs (*OMG! OMG! OMG!*).

WHERE TO FIND THEM

Celebs are like regular people. So says *US Weekly* in the section that shows how famous people pick up their dogs' poop, take yoga classes, eat chili dogs from food trucks, etc. just like we do.

And even the biggest ones can be seen at the most mundane places. They are routinely hiking along public trails, they take meetings in coffee shops, they shop at Whole Foods, and they frequent bars. Where are some popular places to see them?

- Hiking Trails
- Upscale and private gyms
- Nice restaurants
- Coffee shops

- Pacific Palisades, Malibu, the Hills
- Delis
- Sunset Strip
- Supermarkets (you'd be surprised how many gazillionaires do their own shopping)
- Movie Theaters
- Stuck next to you in traffic
- Retail shops
- Basically everywhere but the library and the DMV

Most stars will merely cause you to shrug and make a mental note that you saw them. I'm the guy who misses them completely, so what do I know? I've even had conversations with stars before and not even known I was talking to them. And that was when I *knew* who they were. "Wait, when you introduced her as so-and-so, I didn't know you meant *that* so-and-so." I'm kind of an idiot when it comes to celeb recognition.

Sometimes paparazzi will alert you that the person is famous.

FILMING ON LOCATION

You may already know this, but they do some filming on location in Los Angeles. Any of these shoots can be accomplished on a sound stage or at one of the major studio backlots. Or it might be in your neighborhood. It might even be in your building. You will see large trucks set up on the side of the road, and a security officer just standing there, bored out of their mind. Before this happens, you'll see a "Notice to Film" posted on nearby establishments.

Yes, you may catch a glimpse of one of your favorite stars, but sitting around waiting for that isn't something you should waste your time doing. As you may know, production is like a baseball game — 90% nothing happening.

APPROACHING THEM

NEVER approach them as a fan when you are working on a set or somewhere on the job. You can certainly have a conversation with them if you find an opening, but your first priority is to *do your job*. Even in terms of acceptable work conversation or small talk in passing, do not seek them out as they may be "in their head". Perhaps at the craft service table, but do so in a nonchalant way. If they sense giddiness and fandom, they may recoil. This is, after all, their safe space.

As someone on the crew, you are a co-worker to them. Do not sneak a photo, do not squeal when you shake their hands, and do not stammer when talking to them. If this will be a problem, then don't go near them.

I'm not saying they are all like that. In fact, smaller actors can be quite talkative. But always err on the side of caution. It's similar to the rules of tweeting. This can sometimes wreak havoc with your brain if you're a big fan.

(That said, as the story goes, Ed Burns was working as a PA for *Entertainment Tonight* when he gave Robert Redford a finished video tape of his movie *The Brothers McMullen*. It turned out fine for him, thus proving that there should be no absolutes.)

If they are out and about, they are probably not averse to being spoken to unless they are wearing sunglasses and a hat. Feel the conversation out to see if they'll allow you more than pleasantries.

No need to gush. Keep it short and sweet. (A simple *"I love your work"*, instead of *"I'm a huge fan"* makes you seem more professional.) Something specific is even better. *"I thought such and such was really well done."* The more obscure the work, the better. And don't say it in a creepy way.

I just saw someone, a smaller star, who was in an indie movie I enjoyed. I stopped her as she walked by and said, "Hi, I'm Andy. I just saw you in *The Oranges* and really enjoyed it."

"Oh, great."

"You did a great job."

"Thanks."

And that was it. She walked off and I turned back to my friend. Nothing awkward, nothing too unsettling. Had I wanted a photo, I could have asked.

Treat them as if they are a regular person (imagine that!). If you were in the checkout line at Whole Foods, you could turn to them and refer to the impulse buy section, *"Ah, they have chocolate AND caramel in a wafer now! I can die happy."* (Probably best not to refer to the tabloids or other fluff rags because you never know if they're on it or if one of their friends is mentioned.)

Don't accost them with a script you've written that they'd be perfect for, but you can mention it to them. (At worst, they'll say no. At best, they might tell you to send it to their agent or manager.)

And please avoid making it seem like you are *with* a tabloid. *"Ohmigod! Did you and Jennifer Aniston get along during that movie? I heard she vomits before every scene."* (She doesn't, but who knows what rumors you've heard and believed?)

It takes a little practice to get a decent feel of when to go up to them. When I worked at a network, I approached a showrunner who was waiting in the reception area flipping through a magazine, so I didn't think it would be intrusive. I told him the story of the time I was asked for an autograph of the star of his show, whom I resembled. And the showrunner was quite friendly.

The receptionist did warn me not to do that again, though. Technically, he was right, for you never know if someone (the celeb perhaps?) will say something about you and then you're out looking for work faster than you can say, *"Hey, aren't you the guy from that televi-?"*

Of course, everyone has their "binkie," that one person who, no matter what you're doing – performing CPR on your dying grandma, setting the world's record for balancing plates on your head, or stopping terrorists from taking over the nuclear power plant – will drop EVERYTHING to meet this person and become a fool in the process.

Even stars get starstruck. Backstage at a network affiliates convention, where the new season of a TV shows is celebrated, I watched as one of the highest paid sitcom stars of all-time blathered endlessly to one of his idols, Dick van Dyke.

I have had my moments of saying stupid things (Bruce Willis), speaking overly quickly like a dope (Dave Matthews), and then there were times I was cool and had great conversations and a few memorable photo ops (Dennis "Mr. Belding" Haskins, Fran Drescher, Ray Romano, and many others).

Don't worry. You'll get your stories if you're out here long enough.

WATCH YOUR TONGUE

Whether you are tweeting about something or saying it in a public place, be careful. You can get in trouble real fast with something that everyone does all the time — bad mouth movies or talk smack about actors. In Hollywood, you never know who is around you, or who knows whom. The walls have ears and it's a small town.

One story I heard early in my residence here was about my friend Ryan who was sitting at a restaurant with a friend of his. His friend started bashing Kate Capshaw. Ryan turned white as he saw the diner in the booth behind his friend turn around. Upon seeing Ryan looking ashen, his friend then turned and found himself face to face with Ms. Capshaw's husband – Steven Spielberg.

Uh oh! Now, what's Steven gonna do? It's more embarrassing than anything, but you never know when you might work on a project with him and he remembers your face. (Not sure how it ended for the guy but needless to say, it was not his finest hour.)

Posting on social media can come back to haunt you as well. Remember, your Facebook page and Twitter feed enhance your resume and prospective employers check them. What if you've said something about a show they work on or a celebrity that they are friends with? That could be the end of your shot at working with them.

You can still bash anyone and everyone, just do it in a safe and isolated place, a "zone of privacy," so to speak. This is somewhere you can bash and cajole anything without the possibility of repercussions should your comments get out. You see public figures get in trouble all the time. Even though you're not a public figure, it can still be harmful since we live in this age of social media. (To paraphrase the saying that's as old as the hills: "If you have nothing good to say, don't say it on social media.")

CONCLUSION

Lots of stars live in the Los Angeles area. The tabloids aren't kidding that they're just like us. You should treat them as such. If you are trying to make it in the industry, believe it or not, you are now their peers. You can still be a fan, but a toned down version of one. Prepare yourself for that day you are working with them.

Polite conversation is acceptable, if the moment calls for it. But if you have to gush, do it in the right context, maybe at an awards party dinner and not in line at the pharmacy as one of you fills out an embarrassing prescription.

A helpful rule of thumb is if you have a loud voice and are prone to unapologetic criticism, you should take a moment to scan your surroundings to see who is around you at any public locale.

CHAPTER 14 - TRIPS AND VISITS

INTRO

Hollywood provides the belief that anything can happen to your career at any moment. The carrot dangles flirtatiously just out of reach. That first break can come tomorrow, whether out of the blue or through years of dedication. The last thing you want is to leave town and miss that break. But you must. Otherwise, you will go crazy . . . well, crazier than you are.

HOMESICKNESS

It will take a few years, on average, before you begin to feel at home in Los Angeles. Even then, you'll complain about things and wish it were more like your former home. This is especially true for New Yorkers. Los Angelenos will tell you that New York ranked as the least happy city in America. New Yorkers will tell them that they just don't understand the energy of the "greatest city in the world," only in much more colorful language.

So when do you begin to let yourself succumb to a tinsel existence? Eventually, you'll frequent places you like and avoid places you don't, whether that be the 405 on Fridays, the Viper Room, the beach, or the Starbuck's on 26th and Wilshire because of the crazy couple clad in bathrobes that hangs out there.

VISITING BACK HOME

First rule of vacationing: You'll always miss something when you go away.

Second rule of vacationing: It's never the final straw when you miss something.

For your sanity, you need to get out of town, even if it means giving up something you've been hoping for (which will inevitably come up at the last minute after you've made plans). Remember that Los Angeles is a marathon, not a sprint, so if something passes you by, you'll be able to pick up the race shortly after recharging your batteries. (If, ultimately, you only get that one shot at success, then this is not what you were meant to be doing, so don't feel bad because you chose to attend your favorite cousin's wedding over a callback for a regional non-union commercial.)

Let's say your family is still putzing around your ol' hometown. And let's say you're on good terms with them. Your family loves seeing you. (Though many times, not enough to visit you in Los Angeles.) *When are you coming home? We miss you. It's your cousin's birthday. Your nephew just turned one and asks about you every day.* (Sure, he does.) These are things you might hear from time to time. And every few months you might make a trip. It's easy and it keeps you grounded, but you didn't come out to California to travel back home all the time.

Aside from taking up your valuable time, it can get pricey, and trips to the East Coast take up a full day. (Those outside the country take up even longer.) If you travel via the "red eye," and can sleep on a plane, you can enjoy some daylight upon arrival, followed by a nice meal. The later you leave in the morning, or afternoon, the more likely it is that you'll be picked up from the airport and go right to bed.

The holidays are a good time to spend with your family or friends in other cities, but you must know that it is the worst time to travel. If you're okay with overbooked flights and stressed travelers ready to explode, then by all means, go for it. The city slows down from Thanksgiving through about a week before Christmas, when it becomes a ghost town through New Year's Day. (I.e. that's the BEST time to live here, *hands down.*) The industry is also slower in June and July until about mid-August, kinda like school.

Your Celebrity Status

Traveling home is as close to being on the talk show circuit as you'll get for a while. You are a celebrity! Hometown folk don't know many people who were bold enough to do what you did, which is to drop everything and move to Los Angeles. (Believe me, if you had dropped everything and moved to Tucson, the interest wouldn't be the same.)

153

So you are invited around town, squeezing in as many visits as you can to friends and family clamoring to see you and pick your brain about the experience. You'll notice that the same questions come up over and over, as if you're doing a press junket for your latest feature.

- *Do you see any celebrities?*
- *What's it like living in Hollywood?*
- *Are you famous yet?*
- *When are you moving home?*
- *Do you go to the beach all the time?*
- *Is it crazy there?*
- *Do you see any celebrities? (They'll ask you that one twice.)*
- *What celebrities have you seen?*

It's actually kinda cool. *"Harold, get in here, Alison is about to tell us about the time she saw Michael Douglas coming out of a store on Rodeo Drive. Can we get you some more tea, Alison?"*

People back home will NOT understand quite exactly what life is like in Tinseltown. First of all, we don't call it Tinseltown. We've never even *seen* tinsel. Outsiders think that because they read *People* magazine and *US Weekly*, they get it, but really the city is an enigma. You're their Sherpa and must take them behind the curtain.

You'll astound them with tales of standing in line at the coffee shop in front of John Cusack. *Really? What's he like?* "Seemed nice. He dropped a dollar on the ground. I picked it up and gave it back to him." *What'd he say?* "Thank you." *Whoa! I knew he was the kinda guy that would say that.*

Are you famous yet? is a line you'll hear over and over. Consider that a lot of the things you've accomplished may not seem impressive to you, but are immensely so to them. You can have some fun with this.

In order to live up to their expectations and perhaps feed your ego a little bit, you'll drink. The more you drink, the better your accolades will become.

One drink — *I'm a page at the network.*
Three drinks — *I'm an executive assistant at the network.*
Five drinks — *I'm a vice president at the network!*
Eight drinks — *I OWN THE NETWORK!*

On a side note, a friend of mine from Wisconsin used to tell me this is what he would do and now, a few years later, he's third in command at a major network, so you never know.

The Change in You

Living in Hollywood will change the way you see things in some imperceptible way. It used to be that you would go to a movie, watch it, and then leave the theatre. That was then. Now, in Los Angeles, people congregate outside the theatre for the post-mortem. *What'd you think of the movie?* takes on a whole new significance.

A dissertation will commence. You'll talk about the third act, the resolution, the set design, the casting choice, and stuff you never cared about before, let alone even considered. Your friends from back home don't care about any of this. And they may have liked the movie at which point you'll say, *"What?! Are you serious? It was so derivative. The MacGuffin was contrived and the actor's performance was so bland, I found it hard to focus. I mean, really, I've seen junior thesis projects that were more engaging."* Try not to be too much of an entertainment snob around your hometown folk, but it's difficult now that you've been immersed into the culture for a while.

And if a movie or show takes place in Los Angeles, you'll discuss sights in the movie that you recognized and have been to and/or if there are any continuity errors.

Eventually, your small town perceptions will make way for a more technical and critical view of television and movies.

DAY/WEEKEND GETAWAYS

The moment you are out of Los Angeles County, things change. Not only does the air seem different (i.e. cleaner), but the energy changes as well. They say, "A day in [insert name of a city outside Los Angeles County] is like a week out of Los Angeles."

Here are a few places within the confines of the state that provide ample opportunity for a little break.

Catalina

Catalina is a nice little spot. It's an island about 22 miles off the coast of Los Angeles. It's peaceful, it's quiet, and the ferry to get there allows you a chance to take a break and unwind. (Let someone else do the driving for once.) You can literally feel the congested urban sprawl fading into the background as the cool mist sprays in your face and dolphins play in the boat's wake.

It provides hiking, snorkeling and scuba, among other activities in nature, and a nice little village of shops and restaurants. I have no idea how the place thrives as an actual place where people live, but it does.

This also tells you how to get there by every method except swimming. (If swimming *is* your desired method of travel, then go to the ocean and start kicking your legs and rotating your arms toward the big land mass ahead of you.)

Santa Barbara

Not two hours north on the 101 (which is really west on the 101) lies Santa Barbara. It's near wine-country and has some great wine-tasting rooms, some historic architecture, and an artist's vibe. It has a small city feel to it, but is not too congested.

Also, check out nearby Solvang, a Danish community. How the Danes ended up in California, I have no idea, but they have got great ebelskivers.

San Diego

Founded by the Germans, in 1904, they named it "San Diahgo" which means . . . Sorry, *Anchorman* was on TV as I was writing this.

Just down the coast, about two and a half hours as the crow drives (even the crow has a car), is San Diego. It's relaxing, and lacks all the pretense of Los Angeles. People just love the weather. It's sun and surf all the way. The hustler attitude of Los Angeles is replaced with a genuine laidback appeal. Otherwise, it's pretty nondescript down there.

The city itself is fairly bland for a big city. It's not of the "get out and see things" variety. It has an outdoor mall (Horton Plaza), some nightlife (the Gas Lamp district), Seaport Village, a zoo, Sea World, and Coronado Island. Mainly, you'll go there to relax.

About an hour north on the 15 (only slightly out of the way on your trip home) is Temecula, a growing wine country.

Palm Springs

An oasis in the desert (though still very much the desert) is Palm Springs, the upscale community that is equally high-priced and warm. It typically reaches around 120 degrees in the middle of summer. That's Fahrenheit, though it might may feel like it's Celsius. Sinatra used to have a place there, Liberace as well, and countless other big names.

Located about two hours east, Palm Springs represents the Hamptons for Los Angelenos. They have casinos and showbizzy-type entertainment, like concerts and stand-up performances. It's there to give you a break from LA, yet provides you with many of the perks.

San Francisco

San Francisco falls under what is considered "Northern Cal" even though it's really closer to the middle of the state. (Nobody ever thinks about the *actual* Northern Cal, nor needs to know about it, unless you pick your marijuana directly from the fields or have as much of an affinity for redwood forests as Woody Guthrie.

For the second major city in California, this one is an entirely different world. It's almost seven hours by car. If you were on the East Coast, you would pass a dozen metropolitan areas in that time, but there's very little along the road to San Fran. You can take the 5, which is nothing but farms and slaughterhouses, or the more scenic 101 freeway overlooking the beautiful coastal shoreline, but this takes a little longer.

Whereas the feel of LA and San Diego are fairly similar with their sun-soaked skin and demeanor, San Francisco has an entirely different personality and view of the world.

If you plan to visit in the summer, pack a sweater as you would think you have switched hemispheres. As Mark Twain once said, "The coldest winter I ever spent was summer in San Francisco."

The original wine country is up there – Sonoma and Napa Valleys.

And then there are a couple of spots located just outside the state line which may lure you away.

"The City of Sin" (See: *Vegas, Las*)

Otherwise known as . . . VEGAS!!! For many, the best part of living in Los Angeles is the close proximity to Las Vegas. For all the places difficult for you to get to by being so far out west, Vegas is your savior. It's the popular destination for your friends' bachelor and bachelorette parties and the like and you have the easiest access to it. While they have to change time zones, you merely have to hop a shuttle to get there.

Vegas is a weird place in that there is so much to do to keep you busy for day and you love it, but then, after 24 hours, you feel burned out, ready to go home. The "24 hour turnaround" is a very popular trip. Rent a car, pile a few of your friends in, and go.

By plane, it's a quick hour, barely enough time to get blitzed. Even considering the time it takes to get to the airport and go through security, etc., it's still less than four hours from your place to the craps table.

If you drive, you should be wary of the potential for traffic. It'll take about four and a half hours driving at normal speeds. (And far longer than that on the road home after losing at the craps table.) However, coming back on a Sunday afternoon or at the tail end of a holiday can double that. Eight hours is not unheard of (which is like a full 24 hours in your head when you consider said gambling losses).

Tijuana

If you've made it to San Diego, why not just go all the way to the border where you'll hit Tijuana? Some people love it down there (though I have never found the draw). It's not what you'd call the most alluring of Mexican cities but, again, for a weekend, it's easy access for you.

Bring your passport and some loose change to buy Chicklets.

LONGER TRIPS

And for those longer trips when you really need a break, living in California makes it easier to get to Hawaii and Australia if that's your cup of tea, but the rest of the world is soooo far away. If you want to go to Europe, you end up flying over the North Pole, or thereabouts. Even Santa thinks, "Man, that's a long flight." Just expect to spend a long time on a plane for most places relative to the rest of the country. But that shouldn't extinguish your yearning to see the world.

If you do take a long trip, here are some flight times to get there (all times approximate*):

- Beijing, CHINA - 13 hours
- Berlin, GERMANY - 12 hours
- Cancun, MEXICO - 4 hours, 45 minutes
- Chicago - 3 hours, 30 minutes
- Florida (Miami) - 4 hours, 30 minutes
- Honolulu - 5 hours, 20 minutes
- Jerusalem, ISRAEL - 15 hours, 30 minutes
- Johannesburg, SOUTH AFRICA - 21 hours, 15 minutes
- London, ENGLAND - 11 hours, 30 minutes
- Madrid, SPAIN - 12 hours, 10 minutes
- Moscow, RUSSIA - 12 hours, 40 minutes
- Mumbai, INDIA - 18 hours
- New York City - 4 hours, 45 minutes
- Paris, FRANCE - 11 hours, 50 minutes
- Rio de Janeiro - BRAZIL - 13 hours
- Rome, ITALY - 13 hours, 10 minutes
- San Jose, COSTA RICA - 6 hours
- Seattle - 2 hours, 15 minutes
- Stockholm, SWEDEN - 11 hours, 30 minutes
- Sydney, AUSTRALIA - 15 hours, 30 minutes
- Tehran, IRAN - 15 hours, 40 minutes
- Tokyo, JAPAN - 11 hours, 30 minutes
- Toronto, CANADA - 5 hours
- Trinidad and Tobago - 8 hours, 20 minutes
- Zurich, SWITZERLAND - 12 hours, 20 minutes

*flight times according to www.travelmath.com

ENTERTAINING GUESTS

At some point, you might have friends and/or family come out to see you so prepare yourself to be the most gracious, engaging host/hostess and social coordinator. Los Angeles has a lot of things for your guests to do. That said, one might burn out after four or five days of "cool Hollywood things" to do after the basic Universal

Studios tour, *Price is Right* taping, and walking along Rodeo Drive. Then the visit becomes more typical, one of dinners and sitting by the hotel pool.

There's down time to be had for those coming from bad weather, or you can direct them to one of your favorite out-of-town spots we just learned about.

Here are some of the *in town* crowd-pleasing basics:

- Studios (Universal, Paramount, Sony, Fox, Warner Brothers) have tours
- Networks (CBS, NBC) have tours
- A taping of the legendary *Price is Right*
- See a taping of a sitcom or talk show at one of the studios
- Magic Castle
- Hollywood Boulevard
- Rodeo Drive
- Venice Beach
- The Grove
- A high-priced restaurant with the potential for star-spotting

And that's about it. If you have guests visit regularly, you may find yourself hard pressed to show them someplace new. By then, you can just flip through the entertainment pages for some special event to attend (my parents were in town once for Tim Robbins interviewing Harry Belafonte at the Aero Theatre), or bring them to a favorite spot of yours that they don't have back home.

CONCLUSION

You're human. Part of what will make you more productive is, ironically, the time off to recharge your batteries. If a bender in Vegas is what just what Dr. Feelgood prescribed, do it.

Don't worry about what you might miss out on, but rather what you might be doing to your sanity by staying put on the puree setting that is the blender of LA.

And when people come to visit you, if you're their guide, have a few stand by activities that always seem to impress. Enjoy these moments. And spend some of your own free time acting like a tourist as well. Don't be one of those people who realizes they have not explored the city or region just a few months before you plan to move away.

CONCLUSION

So there is your tour of the Real Hollywood. Have you found it to be more cynical or realistic? There's not much realism in Hollywood, so let's just chalk it up to "it is what it is". I hope you have not been scared off. I tried to make it as practical and hopeful as possible.

Hope for the best and expect the worst has been my motto so that I'm never disappointed. Although it's been extremely frustrating at times, I've found my happiness. As you prepare to take Los Angeles by storm, this guide will help you understand and appreciate the task at hand. Feel free to document your own experiences as you achieve swift and total success. It'll make a great book of its own, I'm sure.

The thing to remember is that this is all a matter of perception. This book comes from living, breathing, talking, and sleeping Los Angeles and the culture for two decades. It comes from commiserating with friends about these very topics. So if you prepare for this lifestyle based on what I've written and are pleasantly surprised to find it's nothing like this book, then I'll be happy to buy you a drink and apologize . . . but let's do it on the Westside . . . sometime after 8 so rush hour will die down.

Your success in Hollywood takes a village and requires a multi-pronged attack of promotion, creation, and development. In fact, it may be *most* important to promote yourself. Social media has made things easier than ever before, from keeping in touch to singing your praises. You are now auditioning every time you post on Facebook and Twitter. Yes, technology has made this easier, but it's also more difficult.

To paraphrase *Glengarry Glen Ross*, "Always . . . Be . . . Creating." You are CEO of your own corporation so present the best, most professional company to the public, even before you hit the NYSE.

Prepare to work. It's not work that is hard, but it's hard work. Set yourself into routines that will put you in the best position to succeed. Be smart and precise about it. Tell the world who you are and get them interested in *getting in bed with you*. (That's just an expression, but if you want to play that literally, that's fine too.) Whet their appetite, so to speak. They'll know if you're the real deal or not, so no need to act like your own mother and oversell your qualities.

There's so much more to this book that needs to be imparted to you, but that's the nuts and bolts of it. This stuff should get you through the first month or so. Then, you're on your own. Find your own truth. At least now you won't be shocked when you get here.

The move will test who you are and you'll come out a different, hopefully truly fulfilled person, both as an artist, and a human being, even if you stop calling people back and use phrases you don't mean such as "a.s.a.p.".

Oh, and just to leave you with something. . .

MY TOP 6 RULES (for what it's worth):

NETWORK – Meet everybody and don't burn bridges until you get to Charlie Sheen's level. Here are a few places to help you get started:

- Stage 32 www.stage32.com
- International Screenwriters Association www.networkisa.org
- LA TV Writers Yahoo! Group tvwriters@yahoogroups.com

HAVE FUN – not too much, but enjoy yourself, your time, and ESPECIALLY the process. Why would you continue to do something you weren't enjoying?

WORK HARD – learn your trade. Don't just coast by and expect you're better than anyone else. There are some people who maintain the perception they just stumble upon their success after partying, but that's not you, or you would not be reading this book.

BE IN THE RIGHT PLACE AT THE RIGHT TIME – you may say, how do I know where the right place will be? The point is, just put yourself out there. Eventually, you'll be in the right place.

YOU DON'T KNOW ANYTHING, NEITHER DO THEY – Everyone is guessing! Some people happen to guess right more often than not. Do not put stock in one person's opinion.

DON'T BE A JERK – This is self-explanatory. Yes, you can't be accessible and sweet and accommodating all of the time, but just treat people with the same respect you expect from them, even if it's not reciprocated. You'll have your chance to take them down a peg if they really wronged you.

KEEP A LOT OF BALLS IN THE AIR – but don't spread yourself too thin. This means always have something cooking, so you don't spend all your days wondering and waiting on that one lottery ticket you've got.

(I lied and gave you seven rules. That should teach you not to believe anything anyone in this town says.)

Good luck. Let me know how it goes! If you have any more questions, or seek further guidance, I can be reached at **andy@hollywoodprimer.com**, but please be patient awaiting a reply. It *is* Hollywood, after all.

APPENDIX

These movies and television shows will give you an idea of what Los Angeles is about and who the people are that you'll be seeing and dealing with. You will laugh and be shocked, as you find that many of these characterizations are DEAD ON

- *American Gigolo* - From 1980, it highlights the ups and downs in the life of a male escort in Los Angeles.
- *Artist, The* - A silent film star on his way down meets and falls in love with a young dancer on her way up.
- *Barton Fink* - A typically off-center Coen Brothers movie where a New York playwright is enticed to California to write for the movies and discovers a hellish truth about Hollywood.
- *Big Picture, The* - A Christopher Guest movie that isn't a mockumentary, but is still so relatable about a film school grad that thinks his career is made after his short film wins an award, but discovers Hollywood isn't as easy as it seems.
- *Boogie Nights* - Set in the late 70s, we follow a young man with a huge . . . er, smile. . . and his adventures in the porn industry.
- *Bowfinger* - Steve Martin pokes fun at almost everything about the industry as he stars as a desperate movie producer shooting a film secretly around the biggest star in the world, played by Eddie Murphy (in one of two roles he plays in the film). Rumor has it that the character played by Heather Graham is based on Anne Heche.
- *Boyz in the Hood* - A 90s drama about a group of childhood friends growing up in a Los Angeles ghetto.

- *Chinatown* - An all-time classic about a private detective caught up in a web of corruption centered around the city's water supply. It gives you a feel of Los Angeles in the 70s.
- *Clueless* - A rich Beverly Hills high school student tries to boost a new pupil's popularity. The scene where the new teenaged driver gets on the freeway is a classic.
- *Crash* - It's about Los Angeles citizens with vastly different lives who collide in interweaving stories of race, loss and redemption.
- *Curb Your Enthusiasm* - The all too neurotic life of Larry David in all its brilliance.
- *Down and Out in Beverly Hills* - A rich but troubled family find their lives altered by the arrival of a vagrant who tries to drown himself in their swimming pool. Mid-80s comedy with Nick Nolte, Richard Dreyfuss, and Bette Midler.
- *Entourage* - A very inside TV show about a movie star and the group of friends he hangs out with, you'll get to see how the industry operates at the higher levels.
- *Episodes* - A TV show about a TV show, it stars Matt LeBlanc as a charming, manipulative version of . . . Matt LeBlanc. See the show through the eyes of British outsiders Beverly and Sean Lincoln, the only ones who see how idiotic everything about Hollywood is.
- *Falling Down* - Michael Douglas snaps and wanders the streets lashing out against society. (Give it a few days of traffic jams and you'll begin to relate.)
- *Fast Times at Ridgemont High* - All the characters at a Southern California high school are the focus here including Jeff Spicoli, Brad Hamilton, and Mr. Hand. Sean Penn and Forest Whitaker have since gone on to bigger and better things, but no one upstaged Phoebe Cates and the carrot in this one.
- *Friday* - Ice Cube and Chris Tucker play two guys in Los Angeles hang out on their porch on a Friday afternoon, smoking and looking for something to do. Spend a week with this movie and then watch its sequel *Next Friday*.
- *Grand Canyon* - Don't let the name mislead you, it's about six Los Angeles residents whose lives intertwine. (The Grand Canyon remains in Arizona.)
- *Heat* - It's got DeNiro and Pacino *and* lots of shots of Los Angeles...getting shot up.

- *LA Story* - This isn't about the love story at the heart of it as a "wacky weatherman" tries to win the heart of an English newspaper reporter, but rather it's about all the jokes about Los Angeles that spring from Steve Martin's brilliant mind such as getting in the car to drive two houses down the street, being confused when he feels breasts that are *actually real*, and a certain hilarious scene on freeway.
- *Mulholland Drive* - It's the madness of David Lynch in a story about a woman who gets amnesia after a car wreck on Mulholland Drive and then searches for answers across the city.
- *Player, The* - An inside peak into the stressful and deceitful movie industry that finds a Hollywood studio executive commit the murder of a writer he thought was sending him death threats, only to fend off the police while staying one step ahead of an up-and-coming rival executive out to make hay at the studio.
- *Point Break* - Such a cult classic that they actually stage a live version of this in town with professional actors reading every character except Johnny Utah, the lead played by Keanu Reeves. They leave that to an Average Joe they pick out of the audience. The results are hilarious in this tale of an FBI agent that goes undercover to catch a gang of surfer bank robbers.
- *Pretty Woman* - The film that made Julia Roberts a star as a prostitute who goes from Hollywood Boulevard to Rodeo Drive thanks to benefactor Richard Gere.
- *Singin' in the Rain* - Quite possibly the greatest musical ever, it takes us back to an age in Hollywood when silent pictures transitioned to "talkies".
- *Slums of Beverly Hills* - The lower-middle class area of town circa 1976 is the focus in this one starring Natasha Lyonne.
- *Speed* - (A fantasy about a freeway where you're actually able to go over 40 miles per hour) In the real world, the bomber has set the bomb to activate when the bus goes over 30. (Yeah, that's not ever gonna activate in Los Angeles then.)
- *Sunset Blvd.* - Are you ready for your close-up? This one's on the Top 100 list and speaks of the addiction to fame when a hack screenwriter pens a script for a former silent-film star who wanted to regain the fame she once had.

- *Swimming with Sharks* - The worst case scenario of working with an agent, though surprisingly still grounded in reality.
- *Swingers* - How to find a significant other in the phony pool as Hollywood.
- *TV Set, The* - The frustrating battle between a writer and the network in a movie about the making of a TV show.
- *Valley Girl* - A girl from the valley meets a punk from the city in this early 80s Nick Cage comedy.
- *Volcano* - Wanna see LA covered in volcanic ash? (Huh? Wait, that can't really happen can it?) That's what happens here where Tommy Lee Jones is all that stands between us and a lava bath.

And here are some books that might help you understand this town a little better as your transition into Hollywood player:

- *The Hollywood Way: A Young Movie Mogul's Savvy Business Tips for Success in Any Career*, by Frederick Levy

- *It's All Lies and That's the Truth: and 49 More Rules from 50 Years of Trying to Make a Living in Hollywood*, by Bernie Brillstein and David Rensin

- *Your Hollywood Pro: How to Make It in the Movie Business Without Selling Out*, by John C. Hall

- *103 Ways to Get Into TV (By 102 Who Did, Plus Me): A Practical Post-College Survival Guide for Coming to Los Angeles*, by Jim McKairnes

- *How to Make It in Hollywood*, by Linda Buzzell

And there are many, many more about acting, auditioning, writing for tv, writing for films, networking, and anything else you'll ever want to know about your life and career in Tinseltown. Find them at The Writer's Store www.writersstore.com or Samuel French www.samuelfrench.com, among other retail shops.

Yes, there's a lot of material on the subject, but you won't need to read them all. At least you have started with the right one. Now go out and learn from experience!

ABOUT THE AUTHOR

Andy Wasif has done it all in his two decades here. From years touring the country as a stand-up comedian to training at famed Improv theaters Upright Citizens Brigade and Improv Olympic, to working as everything from producer to actor, executive assistant, network page, comedy teacher, script consultant, joke writer, blogger, and screenwriter. He's written several insightful humor books including ***Adult Puberty*** and *Boston Globe* bestseller ***Red Sox Fans are From Mars, Yankees Fans are from Uranus.*** His latest screenplay ***The 70 Year Itch*** is currently in development.

31091811R00100

Made in the USA
San Bernardino, CA
01 March 2016